AMBASSADOR FOR CHRIST

AMBASSADOR FOR CHRIST

The Life and Teaching of Paul

WILLIAM BARCLAY

THE SAINT ANDREW PRESS

© WILLIAM BARCLAY 1973

*Originally published in 1951 by
the Church of Scotland Youth Committee*

*Revised and republished in 1973
by The Saint Andrew Press
121 George Street, Edinburgh*

ISBN 0 7152 0210 3

For reason of copyright, not for sale in U.S.A.

The lines by G. A. Studdert-Kennedy appearing on page 162
are reprinted by kind permission of Hodder & Stoughton Ltd.

*Printed in Great Britain by
C. Tinling & Co. Ltd, London and Prescot*

CONTENTS

95927

CONTENTS—*Continued*

FOREWORD

It gives me special and particular pleasure to write the foreword to this book.

This is the first book that I ever wrote, and I have always had to it the feeling that a parent has to his firstborn. It is a long time ago since it was written. I know that throughout the years it has been used in Bible Classes in the Church of Scotland. But I am glad that this edition of it will give it a chance to reach a wider public. I hope that teachers will still find it useful, and that it will help people to understand a little more of the life and thought of Paul.

There are words of thanks which I must speak. I cannot write this foreword without my mind going back across the years to Dr. W. M. Wightman, secretary of the Youth Committee of the Church of Scotland, and to Dr. George S. Mills, secretary of the Scottish Sunday School Union. It was they who made possible the original writing of this book. They are both long since gone to their rest, but it gives me joy to put on record again my gratitude to two men who did very much for the young people of Scotland.

I have also to thank Reverend James Martin, B.D., Minister of High Carntyne Church of Scotland, Glasgow, for preparing the book for this edition. I owe him much for his friendship throughout the years, and his kindness and efficiency in taking upon his shoulders the heavy burden of the preparation of this book for its new printing has put me still further in his debt.

It is my hope and my prayer that this little book may do something to make Paul come alive for our day and generation.

University of Glasgow,   William Barclay
Glasgow,
March 1973

To
B. B. and R. B.
for whom and such as whom
this book was written

and to

K. B.
without whose patience
it could never have been
written.

CHAPTER ONE

This was a Man

The amazing increase

Let us begin by setting two very simple facts side by side. The first is this. After Jesus had done his work on earth and had returned to his Father, the total number of his followers amounted to 120 people (Acts 1:15). To that 120 people was entrusted a task that was enough to daunt the bravest heart, for they were told to go out and win every man in the world for Christ. To take nothing but Jews, there were in Palestine at that time about 4,000,000. That is to say of Jews alone fewer than 1 in 30,000 were Christians. Palestine was a little country, not more than 40 miles from west to east and not more than 120 miles from north to south. Out of that little country this insignificant little band of ordinary folk had the duty laid on them of winning the untold millions of the world for Christ.

The second fact is this. In the year A.D. 64 there fell upon the Christians the first of the great persecutions under the Emperor Nero. Tacitus, the Roman historian, tells us that in that persecution "a vast multitude of Christians" fell to the fury of persecution.

How did Christianity ever succeed in speading from little Palestine halfway across Europe to Rome the capital of the world? How did that little band of 120 simple people become part of a vast multitude of Christians? How did the Christians whom you could count by scores suddenly turn into a people whom you could number perhaps by the hundred thousands? Things do not just happen. Every event must have an adequate cause. The explanation of this amazing increase is none other than Paul.

Paul the man

What kind of a man was this Paul? The New Testament does not tell us what he looked like. But about A.D. 160 an Asian Christian wrote a kind of historical novel called "The Acts of Paul," in which he gives a description of Paul's appearance:

"A man of little stature, thin-haired upon the head, crooked in the legs, of good state of body, with eyebrows meeting, and nose somewhat hooked, full of grace; for sometimes he appeared like a man, and sometimes he had the face of an angel."

It is not a very flattering picture—a short, sturdy, bandy-legged, bald, shaggy-eyebrowed figure—but that was Paul.

The man who conquered his handicap

But we know more about Paul than that. We know that all his life he had to struggle against a very serious physical handicap. Every now and again there came on him an illness which prostrated him with pain.

Here is an amazing thing. If we try to count up the miles Paul travelled on his journeys we find they were about 6,000. When we travel we go by train or car or bus or aircraft. Wherever Paul went he had to walk and 6,000 miles is a long walk for a sick man. Or if he was not walking he was sailing in little uncomfortable ships in which we would be almost afraid to put to sea. There is something heroic in the thought of this little Jew tramping all over Asia Minor and half of Europe and all the time with this handicap holding him back, and yet refusing to give in.

The thorn in the flesh

Paul called this handicap his "thorn in the flesh" (2 Corinthians 12:7). That is the way in which the Revised Standard Version translates it; but very likely the Greek word that is translated "thorn" should be translated "stake." It was not just like the pricking of a thorn; it rather resembled some stake turning and twisting in his flesh. Let us see if we can discover what this stake in the flesh was. Paul never tells us directly, so we have to take all the evidence we can find and try to deduce it.

(i) Paul tells us something about it in his letter to the Galatians (Galatians 4:14, 15). He reminds the Galatians that he was ill when he came to see them first and he says that, in spite of that, they did not despise or scorn him. The word used in the Greek for "scorn" literally means "to spit at."

People in those days believed that illness was caused by an evil spirit taking up its residence in a man's body. These evil spirits were dangerous, and people had special signs and gestures which they made to keep them from coming and settling in them. They believed, for instance, that epilepsy was due to an evil spirit being in a man, and when they met an epileptic they always turned and spat because they believed that would keep the evil spirit from coming into them.

So some people think that, because Paul says that the Galatians did not spit when they saw him but received him kindly, he must have had epilepsy. Ordinarily, people would have spat at an epileptic and kept their distance from him. That is quite possible because we know that Julius Caesar, Oliver Cromwell and Napoleon all suffered from epilepsy. Even with a handicap like that a man can be great.

(ii) But Paul says something else to the Galatians. He says, "You would have plucked out your eyes and given them to me." That sounds as if there was something wrong with Paul's eyesight. Perhaps he was dim-sighted and could not see very well. In fact, there is another thing in the letter to the Galatians which might make us think that this was true. Paul did not actually write all his letters. He usually dictated them, then at the end wrote a few lines in which he gave his personal greetings and signed his name.

In Galatians 6:11 Paul writes, "See with what large letters I am writing to you with my own hand." That paints a picture to us of Paul bending close over the paper on which he was writing and sending a message in big sprawling writing because he could not see to write neatly and properly. Perhaps Paul all his life could not see very well. A man can overcome even that handicap. Witness John Milton who, of course, wrote "Paradise Lost" despite being blind.

(iii) One of the oldest stories about Paul's stake in the flesh is that he suffered from blinding headaches. That could easily have something to do with his eyes. But the likeliest thing of all is that Paul suffered from a certain kind of very bad malaria fever which was common in the coastal parts of Asia Minor. People in those days looked on malarial fever as a punishment and a curse sent by God. And the Galatians might very well have refused to have anything to do with Paul as some one cursed by God.

Two modern travellers who have suffered from this kind of malaria tell us what it is like. One says that the headache that comes with it is like a "red-hot bar thrust through the forehead." The other speaks of "the grinding, boring pain in one temple, like the dentist's drill—the phantom wedge driven in between the jaws"—and says that every moment the person who is suffering seems to have "reached the extreme point of human endurance."

So we must think of this man Paul, all his life at the mercy of these blinding headaches and yet refusing to give in. To have travelled 6,000 miles on foot would be a great achievement for anyone but to have done all that journeying with a handicap like that was the work of a real hero and of a soldier who indeed could endure hardness for his captain's sake.

The great man will not let himself be beaten by any handicap. Instead of letting circumstances master him he will master his circumstances. There was a great English statesman called Lord Curzon who had a weakness of the spine which made it necessary for him to wear a steel jacket. Yet he became Viceroy of India and one of our greatest statesmen. When he died, Stanley Baldwin paid this tribute to him. "He pursued a straight course; and all this in face of daily and constant physical suffering. Of that many knew nothing, because it was a thing of which he never spoke. But I have seen him at the Cabinet, I have seen him at a dinner party, and if he were not able to have the necessary cushions to support his back, his suffering would be as the suffering of a man on the rack, and that he fought against day by day." Lord Curzon could be a great man in spite of even that handicap.

There was a very great priest and preacher of the Church of England whom everyone knew as Dick Sheppard. One day he went to a doctor because he was not feeling well and the doctor told him that he would never be well again and that he had a trouble which would certainly kill him. When he got that news, this is what he wrote in his diary. " 'My number is up,' so the doctor said, and yet I expect that I shall live much longer than he prophesies; but still my number is up. How now to go back and be gallant at home? God give me grace for that at least, so that later she (his wife) may say, 'Your father was brave,' and they may still later say, 'We remember how brave father was.' "

One thing we can start by saying about Paul—that he was a man who lived gallantly. Whatever else he was, he was a hero.

CHAPTER TWO

A Hebrew of the Hebrews

Into all the world

If a man is going out into the world to try to win all kinds of people for Christ he must be a very special kind of man. He must be able to meet all kinds of people. He must be quite at home with scholars and with great men; and equally at home with simple, humble people. He must be quite at home in the great houses of rich people; and equally at home in the cottages and the tenements where the poorer people stay. He must be just as much at home with a man of one country as another.

Dick Sheppard was once explaining how it was that so many people of all kinds came to hear him preach, and his explanation was quite simple. He said, "I am not really much of a preacher, but I am a good mixer." Paul was a good mixer. Paul said himself, "I have become all things to all men, that I might by all means save some" (1 Corinthians 9:22).

We must now see how the very circumstances of his birth and upbringing enabled Paul to mix with anyone on an equal footing.

A Hebrew of the Hebrews

First of all we must always remember that Paul was a Jew and proud of it. When writing to the people at Corinth and stating his qualifications to be an apostle, he writes, "Are they Hebrews? So am I. Are they Israelites? So am I. Are they descendants of Abraham? So am I" (2 Corinthians 11:22). When he is writing to his friends at Philippi, he says, "If any other man thinks he has reason for confidence in the flesh, I have more; circumcised on the eighth day of the people of Israel, of the tribe of Benjamin, a Hebrew born of Hebrews; as to the law a Pharisee" (Philippians

3:4, 5). When he is in danger of arrest and is giving an account of himself, his proud claim is, "I am a Jew, from Tarsus" (Acts 21:39). And when he is addressing the mob who are out for his blood, he tells them, "I am a Jew, born at Tarsus" (Acts 22:3). When he is on trial before the Sanhedrin, he says, "I am a Pharisee, a son of Pharisees" (Acts 23:6).

Paul never forgot that God had given the Jews a very special task to do for Him in this world, and he was proud to be a member of the Jewish nation and the Jewish race.

Paul's education

The Jews were always very particular that their children should be well educated. It was their boast that the children "from their swaddling clothes were trained to recognise God as their Father and as the Maker of the world." One of their great scholars said that Jewish children began learning the law so soon that it was printed on their minds and they could never forget it. They had certain sayings which show how important they thought schools and school children were. "The world is upheld by the breath of children in the schoolhouse." "A town in which there is no school must perish." "Dearer to me," says God, "is the breath of school children than the savour of sacrifice."

We know exactly the kind of education that Paul would receive. When he was six years old he would go to school for the first time. Once he had learned to read he would be given little rolls of parchment with certain scripture passages on them, which he would have to learn by heart. The passages were:

i. The Shema (Deuteronomy 6:4–9; 11:13–21; Numbers 15:37–41).

Shema is the Hebrew for "Hear!" And the title comes from Deuteronomy 6:4, "Hear, O Israel: The Lord our God is one Lord." That might be called the creed of the Jews because that was the verse with which every one of their synagogue services began.

ii. The Hallel (Psalms 113–118). Hallel means "Praise God!" These are all praising psalms and the Jews loved to sing them, especially at the Passover.

iii. The Story of Creation (Genesis 1–5).

iv. The Ceremonial Law (Leviticus 1–8).

In addition, Paul would have to search the scriptures until he found what was called "a personal text." That was a text which began with the first letter of his name and ended with the last. For instance, if we were doing this in English, Proverbs 16:18 would be a personal text for Paul—"Pride goes before destruction, and a haughty spirit before a fall."

When Paul was twelve or thirteen years of age he would become what was called "a son of the law." At that age his father would no longer be responsible for him but he would be himself responsible for keeping the law. On the Sabbath nearest his twelfth or thirteenth birthday he would be taken to the synagogue. There he would be called up to the lectern to read one of the scripture lessons for the day. Then he would be asked certain questions to test his knowledge, and, when he had answered satisfactorily, he was no longer a boy but a man.

Paul the Rabbi

Most boys would stop their education then, but Paul did not. He was to become a Rabbi, which is something like a college professor, and for that purpose he would have to go on and take a higher education, which was the equivalent of going to the university today. There he would go on studying the Old Testament, because the Jews had no other book from which they might read. He would be taught to look for meanings in scripture that the ordinary person could not see.

The Jewish Rabbis said that in every passage of scripture there were four different meanings.

i. *Peshat*, which was the literal meaning.

ii. *Remaz*, which was the suggested meaning and which included all the things that the passage suggested to the wise reader.

iii. *Derush*, which was the meaning after the passage had been investigated and the grammar and the syntax and the references and the history had been carefully studied.

iv. *Sod*, which was the symbolic meaning, the special meaning, that could be read into the passage.

The initial letters of these different kinds of meanings, PRDS, are the letters of the Hebrew word Paradise, and only he who could find these meanings and help others to find them would enter into Paradise.

Paul becomes a Rabbi

This intensive study would last until Paul was about twenty or twenty-one and then he would be qualified as a Rabbi and a teacher. But we must note one thing. No Rabbi was allowed to take any pay for teaching.

The Jews believed two things. They believed that no teacher should ever make money out of his students. One of their wise men said to all teachers, "Make not your students an axe to live by them; make them your crown to win glory by them." And they also believed that every man, even the greatest scholar, should have a trade. They had a saying, "Love work." They said, "He who does not teach his son a trade teaches him robbery." "Excellent is the study of the law along with a worldly trade; for the practice of them both makes a man forget iniquity; but all law without work must in the end fail and causes iniquity." So we read of Rabbis who were millers, shoemakers, tailors, bakers, smiths, carpenters and all kinds of tradesmen.

When he had finished his college course, Paul learned to become a tentmaker. He lived in Tarsus in the province of Cilicia. In that province there were herds of a certain kind of goat which bore a special kind of fleece. From that fleece wool was made which was greatly used for tents and curtains and hangings of all kinds, and it was natural that he should learn that trade.

Paul was always proud that he had never taken a penny for preaching the gospel or for teaching people; he was proud that he had earned his living with his own hands. He reminds his people at Corinth that he "did not burden any one" (2 Corinthians 11:9). He reminds the people at Thessalonica that he worked night and day so that he would not be a burden to any of them (1 Thessalonians 2:9). Besides being a great scholar, he was a skilled craftsman and he was proud that it should be so.

No one should ever be ashamed to earn his money with his hands. There is a story which tells of a nobleman in the old days. He had a great castle and kept open door so that anyone could come in at evening time and have a meal at his table. He had only one test. When a man came to his table he said to him, "Show me your hands." If they were soft and flabby, the hands of a man who had never done a real day's work in his life, that man got a low seat at the table. But if they were worn and scarred, the hands of a worker, the man was given a place of honour at the head of the table. Paul would have approved of that.

So now we see that Paul was a pure-blooded Jew and could meet any Jew on terms of equality; and that also he was one of the greatest scholars of his day and could move in any circle with distinction.

Paul the Pharisee

Purely on Jewish grounds Paul had a further and still greater claim to distinction. He had been a Pharisee (Acts 23:6; Philippians 3:5). Of all Jewish religious figures none were so respected as the Pharisees. There cannot ever have been more than six thousand of them all told but, in one sense, however misguided they were, they were the very cream of the Jewish nation.

Who, then, were they? Very often in the New Testament we get two classes of people mentioned together—Scribes and Pharisees. The Scribes were the experts in the Law. When we read the Law in the Old Testament, we find that it consists of great broad principles; and each individual man is left to apply those principles to the detailed actions of life as his common sense and his reverence for God bid him to do. But that was not enough for the more rigorous of the Jews. They wanted these principles worked out in such a way that there was not an action or event in life which they did not cover.

The best way to see what they did is to take an example. In the Ten Commandments, which are the heart and soul of the Law, we have the commandment that forbids any work to be done on the Sabbath. That is a great wide principle, which safeguards at one and the same time the rights of man and the rights of God. But there were those who were not content to leave it as a principle. They asked, "What is work?" They then laid down thirty-nine different kinds of activity, which they called "fathers" of work. Not content with that, they tried to define every possible kind of sub-section of these thirty-nine different kinds of work.

Again, let us take an actual example of the thing in practice. One kind of work was carrying a burden; therefore the carrying of burdens on the Sabbath was prohibited. But that was not enough for these legalists. They went on to ask, "What is a burden?" The answer was, "A burden is anything that weighs as much as one fig." So it was forbidden to wear any kind of brooch or clasp on the Sabbath or even to carry a pin stuck in the coat for that would be to carry a burden. It was gravely debated whether it was right to wear false hair or false teeth on the Sabbath; that might be said to be carrying a burden. It was debated whether a man was carrying a burden if he lifted up his child on the Sabbath. It was conceded that he might do that but, if the child had in his hand a stone, that was carrying a burden. Shoes studded with nails might not be worn on the Sabbath for that would be to carry a burden.

It was considered work to heal anyone on the Sabbath. Therefore if a person had a sore ear, he might wear plain wadding in it but not medicated wadding; for that would have been to help to cure the sore ear, and that would have been to work. If a person was wounded or injured on the Sabbath, unless his actual life was in danger, only a plain bandage might be put on the wound. No ointment and no salve might be applied for that would have been to heal and therefore to work on the Sabbath. It was in consequence of that rule that the Scribes and Pharisees accounted Jesus a sinner because he healed men on the Sabbath day.

There were literally thousands of rules and regulations like that. In addition, there were all kinds of rules about just how often and just in what way the hands must be washed before a meal. In addition to that, the strict legalist would with meticulous care measure out one exact tenth of even his garden herbs to give to God. All life was hedged around by these detailed rules and regulations, which the Scribes had worked out and systematised from the great broad principles of the Law.

The name Pharisee means "the separated one." And the Pharisees were those who had separated themselves off from ordinary folk and ordinary life in order to keep every detail of the Law. The Scribes were experts in what the Law demanded, but they did not themselves strictly keep the Law. The Pharisees kept every littlest detail.

What made things even worse was that the Pharisees would have nothing to do with anyone who was not as strict as they were. They would not have such a one in their house; nor would they enter his house. That is why they condemned Jesus for eating with tax-gatherers and sinners. They would not buy anything from or sell anything to anyone who did not keep these laws. They would not even let the skirt of their robe touch such a person.

Inevitably they were cut off from all ordinary people; and they became spiritually proud until, in actual fact, they did thank God that they were not as other men were. There is a record of a Pharisee who said, 'If there are only two righteous men in the world, I and my son are these two. If there is only one righteous man in the world, I am that man." There was a Pharisaic law, which said of the ordinary man, "Bear no witness for him, take none from him, reveal to him no secret, entrust nothing to his charge, make him not a treasurer of monies for the poor, associate not with him on a journey." They even denied that the common man would have any share in the resurrection from the dead.

It is easy to criticise the Pharisees and to condemn them as misguided and arrogant legalists. But one thing is clear—they must have been desperately in earnest. A life dominated by these rules and regulations must have been a most restricted and uncomfortable thing, and yet of their own free-will they accepted such a life and kept to the utmost its every detailed regulation. Only someone with a fanatical intensity of belief would have attempted that.

Paul was like that. He was a man who had a passion for the Law. He was willing to make life as uncomfortable as its minutest regulations demanded in order to be, as he thought, true to God.

We see how Paul's qualifications to appeal to his fellow-countrymen are piling up. He was a Jew of the purest blood; he was a Rabbi with the highest possible academic attainments; he was a Pharisee, one of that devoted six thousand who, however misguided they may have been, were nonetheless the shocktroops and the spearhead of Jewish religion.

CHAPTER THREE

To the Greeks

The Apostle to the Gentiles
In our last chapter we saw that Paul could meet any of his fellow
Jews on level terms in any sphere of life. In matters of racial
purity, of academic distinction and of religious achievement he
was second to none. But it was not Paul's task to be the apostle of
the Jews. His commission was to carry the name of Christ before
the Gentiles (Acts 9:15). And once again life and circumstances
had peculiarly fitted him for this task.

No mean city
As we saw, Paul, although a Jew, did not come from Palestine
but was a citizen and a native of Tarsus in the Roman province of
Cilicia, one of the busiest cities in the world. It stood on the
Mediterranean Sea, at the mouth of the River Cydnus, and was
one of the world's great ports. Further, it stood at the end of a
road that came all the way across Asia Minor from the far off
Euphrates, and the wealth and the commerce of the hinterland
poured into Tarsus for export. It was one of the most cosmopolitan cities in the world.

When Paul was a boy he must have seen men of all nations
walking the streets in Tarsus from the ships in the harbour and
from the caravans from the interior. If we think of the 6,000 miles
that he travelled for Christ it is clear that Paul was always an
explorer, an adventurer, a pioneer at heart. There was in him
something of the wanderlust. There is a phrase which can be
said to haunt him; it is the phrase "the lands beyond" (2 Corinthians 10:16). A great scholar once said that Paul never saw a
boat riding at anchor in a haven or moored at a quay but he

wanted to board her and to preach the gospel to the lands beyond. He never saw a range of hills blue in the distance but he wanted to cross them and to preach the gospel to the lands beyond.

So we can think of Paul as a boy wandering about the docks, the harbours and the quays of Tarsus, looking with envious eyes at those men who sailed the seas, standing in the streets and watching the caravans and dreaming of the day when he too might go out by the narrow pass into the table lands of Asia Minor, even then haunted by the lands beyond. It would have been difficult for anyone to grow up in Tarsus and not to catch a vision of the size of the world and the varieties of men. It must have been impossible for a lad with the sensitive, vivid imagination of Paul to fail to have his dreams of lands over the hills and across the sea.

But Tarsus was more than a mere commercial city. In Tarsus there was one of the most famous universities in the world. Perhaps it was not just as famous in the academic life as the ancient universities of Athens and Alexandria but the scholars of Tarsus were famous for one thing—a burning and even a passionate enthusiasm for learning. Now Paul was a Jew and the son of a Pharisee. We have seen how the Pharisees could have no contact with those who did not keep the law. Paul could never have been a student at that university nor could he ever have systematically studied Greek learning; but no one could walk the streets of Tarsus or linger in the city squares without over-hearing the conversation of those who talked and argued about all kinds of philosophies and all kinds of problems. Even then the mind of the young Paul must have been forced to think furiously about the greatest things of all.

Paul was a Jew and yet he never forgot Tarsus. When he was accused of being a reckless revolutionary his proud reply was, "I am a Jew, from Tarsus in Cilicia, a citizen of no mean city" (Acts 21:39). Tarsus had a good conceit of herself, for she inscribed upon her coins, "Tarsus, the Metropolis, First, Fairest and Best." And Paul was not above feeling pride that he had been nurtured in such a city.

Here, then, again Paul is winning his qualifications to be the apostle to the Gentiles. True, he is a Jew and proud of it; but he has been born and bred in a city as cosmopolitan as any in the world. A man who grew up in a city like that could say as Terence, the Roman poet, said, "I count no human being a stranger."

The Roman citizen

But Paul was more than merely a citizen of Tarsus, he was a Roman citizen. And he was proud of that. When he was arrested in Philippi and flung into prison and the magistrates proposed to release him and say no more about it, he would not have it that way. "You have beaten us," he said, "and you have imprisoned us and we are Roman citizens; not a foot do we move until you have publicly apologised" (Acts 16:35–39). When he was about to be scourged in Jerusalem, he demanded, "What right have you to scourge a man who is a Roman citizen?" (Acts 22:25). When he was in prison in Rome at the end of his days, he wrote to Timothy, "Bring the books, and above all the parchments" (2 Timothy 4:13). It is most likely that the parchments were his certificate of Roman citizenship. He wanted it then.

At that time all the world was the Roman Empire. From Britain in the west to Persia in the east, from Germany in the north to North Africa in the south, the world was Rome. And, on the whole, the rule of Rome was something for which men were devoutly thankful. As E. J. Goodspeed has written, "The provincial, under Roman sway, found himself in a position to conduct his business, provide for his family, send his letters, and make his journeys in security, thanks to the strong hand of Rome." Rome had banished the pirates from the seas and the brigands from the roads, and had welded the world into one; and Paul was proud to be a Roman citizen.

Furthermore, he was born a citizen (Acts 22:28). There were different ways in which a man might become a citizen. Sometimes whole areas were given the citizenship; veteran soldiers when they had come to the end of their service were given the citizenship; sometimes people bought the right to be citizens; sometimes the citizenship was conferred as a special reward for great service to Rome. However Paul's father won the citizenship, Paul was born a Roman citizen and he never forgot it.

Citizenship conferred certain rights. A Roman citizen could not be imprisoned without a trial; he could never be scourged; and if he was not satisfied with the justice he was getting in some provincial court, he could appeal directly to the Emperor, and the Emperor would personally attend to the complaint of his humblest citizen.

Once again we see how Paul has the qualifications to make him the apostle to the Gentiles. He was a Roman citizen, and wherever he went the majesty of Rome was behind him.

"All things to all men"

Once Paul claimed that he had been all things to all men in order to save some (1 Corinthians 9:22). God in his wise providence had made that possible for him. In regard to the Jews, he was the equal of any in birth, in scholarship and in religion. In regard to the Gentiles, he had been brought up in the most cultured and the most cosmopolitan of cities, and he was a citizen of Rome. God had so ordered Paul's life that he was fitted to go out into all the world and to meet any man on equal terms.

CHAPTER FOUR

In the Fulness of Time

The hour and the man

If great things are to happen two elements are required.

First, it is necessary that there should exist a man who has the qualities of mind and heart and spirit to make him a real instrument in the hands of God. And second, it is necessary that there should exist a set of circumstances which makes it possible for that man to act.

Sometimes there has existed in history a situation which was crying out to be used; but there was no man to use it. And sometimes there has existed in history a man who might have done great things, but who was frustrated because the time was not ripe. If great things are to happen, it is necessary that the man and the hour should come together.

We have seen that in Paul there was a man fitted in the most unique way for the task of bringing the gospel to all the world; but even Paul could not have performed that task as he did, unless the circumstances of the hour had been designed by God to make it possible to carry it out.

One language

One of the basic difficulties of the missionary is that of making himself understood. It will often be necessary for him, if he goes outside the bounds of his own country, to learn a foreign language, and that is no small task. But in the days of Paul that difficulty hardly existed; for nearly all the world spoke Greek.

Almost four hundred years before, there had gone out from Macedonia Alexander the Great. His conquests had extended from Greece to far-off India; and wherever Alexander went he took the Greek language. He said himself that he felt it to be his destiny to wed the East to the West. That is to say he did not look on himself as only a conqueror and a general; but as one whose divine mission it was to spread over all the world the Greek way of life, Greek thought, Greek culture and inevitably the Greek language.

What happened was that people did not stop using their own language; they used their native tongues in the privacy of their own homes and amongst their familiar friends. But in the world of trade and politics and learning they used Greek. We know for instance that Plutarch, the great Greek, came from his home town of Chaeronea on an embassy to Rome and got on very well although he had only the barest smattering of Latin. At least in all the great cities and the great centres everyone spoke Greek.

The situation was very like that which exists in the Western Highlands of Scotland or in Wales to-day. In these parts of Britain some people speak Gaelic or Welsh among themselves; but often in the world of trade and business and public affairs they use English.

One very simple thing shows this actually at work in the New Testament. It is the at first puzzling fact that so many of the characters in the New Testament have two names. The explanation is that one is a Hebrew name by which they were known by their families and their intimate friends; and one is a Greek name by which they were known in public life. Thus Peter is the Greek for "a rock," and Cephas is the Hebrew for the same word. So Thomas is the Hebrew for "a twin," and Didymus is the Greek for the same word. Everyone in those days, who lived in touch with civilisation, spoke Greek.

Think of the vast advantage this gave Paul and his fellow-missionaries. They had none of that difficult task of learning a new language in order to preach the gospel. Wherever they went, they could tell the Good News in Greek, and men would understand.

An audience

Another difficulty the modern missionary has is the simple yet basic one of getting an audience to listen to him. Somehow or other he has to gather a crowd who will listen to what he has to say. Once again that difficulty was solved for Paul and his friends. The centre of Jewish religious life was the synagogue. Wherever there were ten Jewish families, there must be a synagogue. Now there were Jews all over the world. There may have been as many as a million of them in Alexandria; there were tens of thousands of them in Rome. All over the east Alexander had founded new cities; and in almost every one of them he had given the Jews the rights of citizenship, because then, as now, the Jews were the great traders and bankers of the world, and they were useful citizens to have. So in any town of any size there would be a synagogue.

In these synagogues there assembled on the Sabbath days far more than Jews. There were men of many nations who were weary of the worship of a whole host of gods; there were many who were tired of the low moral standards of heathen ways. They found in the one God in whom the Jews believed someone whom they could really worship; and they found in the Ten Commandments and in the Jewish law a code of morals that was a real foundation for life. Some of these people actually accepted circumcision and became Jews; but the vast majority simply came to the synagogue to find out more about the true God and the good life. Those who were actually circumcised and became converts to Judaism were called proselytes; those who came weekly to the synagogue to learn were called god-fearers. So in every synagogue—and there was a synagogue in every town of any size—there was a ready-made audience which included not only Jews but a good proportion of Gentiles too.

We may well ask what good that would be? We very likely think of the synagogue as being like our church; and if a stranger came there he would be made welcome as a member of the congregation but it is unlikely that he would have a chance to address the congregation.

We have to remember two things about the synagogue. First, someone has called the synagogues the popular religious universities of their day. There was far more actual teaching and instruction, and discussion at their services than at ours. Second, the synagogue service gave the early Christian missionaries their chance. It was divided into three parts. The first part was prayer; the second part was reading from the scriptures; and the third part was the address. But the ordinary member of the synagogue had a far bigger part in the service than the ordinary church member. It was members of the congregation who read the scripture lessons; and, what is much more important, there was no one person to give the address. If any distinguished stranger was present, he would be called on to speak; it might even be that anyone who had a message would be invited to give it.

Thus wherever Paul and his fellow-missionaries went they found a synagogue; and wherever there was a synagogue they had a chance to speak. In the services of the synagogue they had their opportunity to state their message and to discuss it not only with Jews but also with Gentiles.

Even outside the synagogue these early missionaries had a chance that modern missionaries do not have. The Greek world worshipped the spoken word and the Greek mind loved nothing better than to discuss some new idea and some new theory. The Greek world was full of wandering preachers. Any man who had a theory to set out and who had some gift of words in which to set it out was sure of an audience. In fact, the great orators were very much in the same position as the entertainment idols of to-day. If it was announced that one of them had booked a hall and would give a lecture, there would be crowds fighting for admission. Nothing was easier than for a wandering preacher to gather a crowd in those days.

Both the Jewish and the Gentile world were such that Paul and his friends would never have the slightest difficulty in gathering a crowd to listen to "the new philosophy" which they wished to teach.

One world

There was yet another priceless element in the world situation for the spread of the Gospel. The world at that time was one world. Let a man travel from Britain and Spain in the west to the bounds of Asia Minor in the east, and wherever he went he was still in the Roman Empire. There were no frontiers; there were no passports needed; there were no iron curtains to penetrate. Nowadays if a man proposed to wander from Britain to Asia Minor he would have to traverse France, Germany, Austria, Italy, Yugoslavia, Greece, Turkey, Iran and many another state.

To make the journey at all he would need a passport. At every frontier he would be held up and examined before he was allowed to pass on; it is extremely probable that a wandering preacher with no visible means of support would not be allowed into half of these countries at all; and there are certain countries which very definitely would not allow a preacher of any kind to cross their borders.

But it was not so in the time of Paul. The world was one world. A man could not get out of the Roman Empire if he tried; and if he was a Roman citizen, as Paul was, he could roam without let or hindrance from one end of the world to the other. Doors that would now be shut were wide open to Paul.

The roads of Rome

Further, Paul lived in a time when travel was easier than it ever had been in the ancient world. From one end of the empire to the other the Romans had built their roads. These Roman roads were built to last for ever. We can see parts of them yet going straight as a die across the landscape. There was the Via Appia, which led from Rome to Capua and then across Italy to Tarentum and Brindisi. If a man wanted to go on further, he would cross the sea to Dyrrachium and then he would be on the Via Egnatia, which ran through the very main street of Thessalonica to Philippi and then on to Byzantium which is now Constantinople; and, if he wanted to go further he could follow that road on through Nicodemia and Ancyra, until it brought him to the Euphrates and the far east. If he wanted to go north from Rome, he could take the Via Flaminia, which would take him to Rimini, Bononia, Milan and round the coast to Marseilles; and if he wanted to go further, he could follow that road north up through Vienna and into what is now central Europe. Or, if he wanted to stick to the Mediterranean, he could take the Via Aurelia which ran right round the coast by Genoa again to Marseilles. If he wanted to go south from Rome he could take the Via Popilia which would take him from Rome to Rhegium in the toe of Italy; and then, if he wished, he could take ship to Messina in Sicily and journey across Sicily to Lilybaeum; and if he wished still further adventures he could take ship again to North Africa and land at Utica near to ancient Cathage.

All over the world went those great roads. It was true that all roads led to Rome; for all along the roads were the milestones which marked out the miles to the golden milestone which stood in the forum in the heart of the capital.

The ancient peoples were not so fond of the sea; but they were seafarers too. Especially they sailed from Rome to Alexandria, for Rome could not live without the corn that Egypt sent. The wind in the Mediterranean blows from the west and the journey from Rome to Alexandria was made direct, slipping past the south of Crete. It took at the most about twenty days. But the passage from Alexandria to Rome was a different question. The sailing ships could not make it direct because of that west wind. So they might try to sail direct to Rhodes; and then slip past Crete round Malea and Cythera, and then across to Rhegium and so up the coast to Puteoli for Rome. Or they might hug the coast up by Caesarea, Tyre and Sidon; across to Cyprus and up to Lycia and then to Rhodes and so on to Italy. That voyage, when the wind was contrary, might take as long as sixty days.

So all over the Mediterranean there sailed the ships from Italy to all the ports.

And these roads and these sea-routes were safe. Less than a hundred years before, the brigands and the pirates had made voyaging a hazardous adventure; but the strong hand of Rome had spread the Roman peace throughout all the world. And the roads to all the world and the ships to all the ports were there for Paul to use.

A world at peace

There was still another circumstance, which greatly helped Paul and the early Christian missionaries. They had the rare experience of having to do their work in a world which was at peace. It has been calculated that in the 3,000 years or so in which men have been writing history there have been fewer than 150 years during which war has not been raging somewhere. Now if Christianity had had to attempt to spread throughout the world amidst wars, the task of the missionaries would have been doubly difficult. If the whole of Europe and of Asia Minor had been involved in wars and battles, it would have been very much harder for the missionaries to pass from country to country. But at that time there was peace. Men still talk of the *Pax Romana*, the Roman Peace. Rome had given peace and order to the world and, by so doing, had all unawares made easier the spread of Christianity throughout the world.

The state of men's hearts

So then Paul and his friends went out into a world where there was one language, where, in the synagogue, there was a ready-made audience, where every street-corner would provide a listening crowd, where there were no political or national barriers and where there was one of the rare periods of world peace. But there were things of even greater help than these. Not only was the state of the world an asset to the spread of Christianity. What was still more important, men's hearts were waiting for that which Christ alone could bring to them.

The top of the social scale

In the Roman Empire there were three levels in the social scale. First, there were the wealthy. It is doubtful if the world ever saw such an age of luxury. They sat down to banquets which cost as much as £6,000, and at which such dishes as nightingales' tongues and peacocks' brains were set before the guests. At one banquet the Emperor Vitellius set on the table 2,000 fish and 7,000 birds. They ate from jewelled dishes of gold and silver which themselves were worth a fortune. Vitellius was Emperor only for about eight months and yet in that short period he spent millions of pounds on food alone. It was during this time that there arose the revolting custom of taking emetics before a meal and even between the courses that the flavour of each dish might be more keenly tasted. It was the same in dress. There is a record of a Roman lady called Lollia Paulina who sat down to her betrothal feast wearing a robe which was so richly wrought and jewelled that it cost over £100,000.

The moral condition of the wealthy part of the Roman world was as low as it could possibly be. Family life had broken up. For the first 520 years of the Roman Empire there had been no such thing as divorce; but now, as Seneca said, "Women married to be divorced and were divorced to be married." In Rome two new consuls were chosen each year and the years were called after the consuls. Instead of saying "in such and such a year", the Romans said, "when so-and-so was consul." There was a bitter saying that Roman women counted the years not by the names of the consuls but by the names of their husbands. To have a family was considered a misfortune, and night after night dozens of little children were found abandoned in the city square of Rome.

One might think that such a state of affairs would be an impenetrable barrier to Christianity. But the very fact that Roman society did these things showed that they were at heart desperately discontented and were looking for something which would give them satisfaction. The greater their luxury and the greater the lengths to which they went in pleasure and in immorality, the greater this longing in their hearts to find some kind of real pleasure in life. They were desperately looking for something which only Christ could give them.

Matthew Arnold wrote a poem in which he describes this state of things:

> On that hard pagan world disgust
> And secret loathing fell;
> Deep weariness and sated lust
> Made human life a hell.
> In his cool hall, with haggard eyes,
> The Roman noble lay;

> He drove abroad in furious guise
>   Along the Appian Way;
> He made a feast, drank fierce and fast,
>   And crowned his hair with flowers—
> No easier nor no quicker passed
>   The impracticable hours.

From the Christian point of view it looked a very daunting world to face, but in point of fact it was looking for something which Christianity alone could bring.

The bottom of the social scale

At the opposite end of the social scale there were the slaves. In the Roman Empire there may have been as many as sixty million slaves. Many of them were kindly treated by their masters and were almost members of the family. But on the whole the fate of the slaves was almost unspeakably hard. In the eyes of the law a slave was not a person; he was a thing. He was a living tool. A slave was defined as a person who belonged not to himself but to someone else. Legally his master could do anything he liked with him and often the masters did. A master could kill or torture his slave and no one could stop him; and the great families numbered their slaves by the thousand.

One Roman writer advises the farmer at the end of each year to take stock of his implements, and, if he finds any old spades or ploughs, to throw them out and not to let them clutter up the place; and if he finds any old broken slaves, who are past their work, let him throw them out and leave them to die.

There is on record a story of a Roman feast which was being held in the courtyard of a Roman house. A slave was serving wine and in so doing slipped and dropped a valuable goblet. In the centre of the courtyard there was a pool filled with savage carp, and the master at once ordered the slave to be thrown into the pool, where in a moment the carp had literally torn him to pieces.

If a slave attempted to run away and was caught—and he had little chance of not being caught—he was branded on the forehead with a red-hot iron with the letter F, the first letter of the Roman word *fugitivus* which means a runaway. Literally the slaves mattered to no one. They were not allowed to marry. If they did live together and a child was born, the child belonged, not to them, but to the master, just as the lambs of the flocks belonged to the owner.

What must it have meant to these slaves, who were not regarded as human beings at all, to hear the message that God loved every man, that every individual was dear to God, that "God loves each one of us as if there was only one of us to love."

Much later in history there was a penniless scholar, called Muretus. As he wandered about seeking for knowledge, he fell ill and was taken into a public institution. The doctors were bending over him and they were discussing his case. They were talking in Latin, which was the language that all scholars used in those days. They were saying that he would not get better anyway, that they would like to carry out some experiments on him, that no one would care what happened to him, for he was an entirely worthless creature. Little did they think that this ragged scarecrow of a man understood what they were saying; but he did and he looked up at them and said, in their own Latin, "Call no man worthless for whom Christ died." The slaves in Rome must have felt when they heard the message of Christianity, that for the first time they mattered to someone—and that someone was none other than God.

The middle classes

In between the wealthy and the slaves there came the ordinary citizens, the middle classes. Now as regards the ordinary man one great tragedy had befallen Rome. Rome was the mistress of the world; and the Roman citizen had come to the conclusion that it was beneath his dignity to work. All the work, therefore, was done by slaves. Even people like teachers and doctors and writers were slaves. And so the ordinary citizen far too often had nothing to do but lounge about. Usually he became the client of some wealthy patron. The very wealthy sought to get themselves honour and fame by the number of clients they supported; and the ordinary man would turn up at his patron's great house in the morning to pay his respects and to get his dole for the day, and then go off to stand at the street corners or in the city squares.

These people had to be kept amused and it was for them that the gladiator games were run. Sometimes the gladiators were slaves; sometimes they were reckless free men, the kind who in later time would have joined the French Foreign Legion. Sometimes they were even wealthy aristocrats, for a gladiator in Rome could be as famous as a bullfighter in Spain today. Sometimes they fought against each other; sometimes against wild beasts; sometimes they were armed with swords and sometimes all they had to defend themselves was a net like a fishing net and a trident. As they marched into the arena, they faced the mob and said, "We who are about to die salute you." The Emperor Augustus in his will claimed to have put into the arena during his reign no fewer than 8,000 gladiators and 3,510 wild beasts. Later we are told of 11,000 beasts and 10,000 men having to fight. In a sham sea-battle we are told that 19,000 men fought against each other.

We may think that it would be impossible to sit and watch men hacking each other to pieces or being devoured by wild beasts. People may have felt like that on their first visit to the arena, but soon the hysterical excitement gripped them and they were mad with the lust for blood.

Once again, the fact that people crowded to these games shows how desperately they were seeking satisfaction. They had nothing to do, and they had to find some kind of sensation which would give them a thrill. They had nothing in which they could invest their lives; once again, although they did not know it, they were waiting for what only Christianity could give them. The moral condition of the world might look completely discouraging; but in reality it provided just that challenge and that chance which Paul and his friends needed to spread Christianity amongst all men.

CHAPTER FIVE

A New Creature

Paul the persecutor

We have seen how Paul was peculiarly fitted by the training and the experiences of his life to bring the story of Jesus to all the world; and we have seen how the circumstances of the world were such that the stage seemed set for the spread of Christianity. But there was a time when nothing seemed less likely than that Paul should be the missionary of Christ. There was a time when his one ambition was to obliterate the memory of Jesus Christ from the world and to eliminate the last Christian who might survive. There was a time when Paul the apostle to the Gentiles was Paul the persecutor.

That was a period in his life which he could never forget. It was burned into his memory and time and time again he mentions it with shame and with bitter regret. In Acts 8:3 it is said of him that "he laid waste the Church." The word used is very vivid. It is the word used of the damage that a wild boar did when he got into a vineyard. Just as a wild boar left a trail of utter destruction, so Paul acted towards the Christians and the Church with all the savagery and ferocity of a wild animal.

When Paul did in the end submit to Christ, the Christians said in incredulous amazement, "Is not this the man who made havoc in Jerusalem of those who called on this name?" (Acts 9:21). Again the word used is vivid. It is the word used for an army sacking a city. Just as an invading army might tear a city stone from stone and murder and slaughter right and left with almost sadistic brutality, so Paul had attacked the Christian Church.

In his letters Paul shows how these memories of his persecuting

days still stabbed his conscience. When he is writing to the people
of Galatia, he says, "You know how violently I persecuted the
Church of God, and tried to destroy it" (Galatians 1:13, 23).
Again he uses that word which is used of an army sacking a city
and another word which might be used of a hunter hunting down
his prey. When he writes to the Corinthians, he tells them that at
the best he is fit to be called only the least of the apostles and that
at the worst he is not fit to be called an apostle at all, because he
persecuted the Church of God (1 Corinthians 15:9). At the very
end of his days, when he is writing to Timothy, the same bitter
thought is still with him. He talks of himself as one who "for-
merly blasphemed and persecuted and insulted" Christ Jesus (1
Timothy 1:13). The word he uses for "insulted" is again a vivid
word. It means that he arrogantly set himself up as judge and
executioner of the Christian Church.

Not only does this memory emerge in his letters; it emerges in
his speeches, too. When he was facing in Jerusalem the mob out
for his blood, he told them that once he had "persecuted this way
to the death, binding and delivering to prison both men and
women" (Acts 22:4). When he was making his speech to King
Agrippa in Caesarea he said, "And I punished them often in all
the synagogues, and tried to make them blaspheme; and in raging
fury against them, I persecuted them even to foreign cities."
(Acts 26:11). At one time there was in Paul's heart a rage and a
bitter hostility against Jesus Christ and all that he stood for,
that drove him on to a career of persecution, which had the one
object of wiping the name of Christ from the earth.

Why did Paul hate Christ so much?

We are bound to ask why Paul hated Jesus and all that he stood
for so much. There were two reasons. The first was that *Jesus
claimed to be the Messiah of God*. The Jews had always looked on
themselves as God's chosen people. They thought of themselves
as standing in a specially privileged position in regard to God.
They dreamed of a day when, because they were God's people,
they would be the greatest people in all the world. Their history
did not look as if that was true, because they had been subject in

turn to the Babylonians, the Persians, the Greeks and the Romans. There were so few of them and their territory was so small, that, humanly speaking, it looked impossible that this long dreamed of greatness should ever materialise. So the Jews had come to the belief that what could not happen by human means was bound to happen by divine means; and they dreamed of a day when God's Messiah would come. Messiah is the Hebrew and Christ is the Greek for "The Anointed One." When kings were crowned they were anointed with oil and therefore Messiah or Christ really means "God's Great King."

There were different ideas of what this great king would do when he came. Sometimes people thought of him as a conquering hero, who would lead the armies of the Jews throughout the world, who would batter the Romans into subjection and go from conquest to conquest until the whole world was an Empire over which the Jews would rule supreme. Sometimes this involved the utter destruction of every Gentile in all the world; sometimes it involved the reducing of the Gentiles to the position of slaves of the Jews; sometimes—but this did not happen very often and it had not entered into Paul's mind at all at first—it involved the converting of the Gentiles into the love of God. In any event, this Messiah King was to be a mighty conqueror.

As for this Jesus—this pretended Messiah—had he not ended upon a cross as a criminal? To make it worse the Jewish law itself said that the man who hung upon a cross was accursed of God (Deuteronomy 21:23). To Paul it was the final blasphemy that a man who had been crucified could ever be held to be the Son of God and the Messiah King. To translate the idea into modern terms, it was like taking a convict, sentenced to death for some grim and revolting crime, and asking people to believe that this man alone had spoken the truth and that he alone must be taken as the master of life. To Paul the whole basis of Christianity was a pernicious and a blasphemous lie, which must be stamped out as completely and as quickly as possible.

The second reason which drove Paul to seek to eliminate the name of Jesus from history was the fact that, *if Jesus was right about God and the good life, then Paul and every orthodox Jew were wrong.* The basis of orthodox Jewish thought was that if men kept the Law then they pleased God. If they prayed every day at 6 a.m., 9 a.m., 12 midday, 3 p.m., and 6 p.m.; if they observed the Sabbath Law with all its petty details; if they washed their hands in the right way at the right time; if they gave tithes of every littlest garden herb to God; if they had nothing to do with anyone who did not keep this Law; then, they believed, they were pleasing God.

Now Jesus broke that ceremonial law right and left. He allowed His disciples to pluck ears of corn on the Sabbath and so to work and therefore to sin. He himself healed people on the Sabbath and so worked and therefore sinned. He did not observe all the ceremonial of handwashing and the like and was therefore a sinner; he companied with people, who were tax-gatherers and sinners and who lived the most immoral kind of lives, and was therefore a sinner. The fact that he healed the sick and comforted the sad and brought back the outcast and taught men to love each other was nothing to men like Paul whose one passion was the Law. What made it worse was that the Rabbis had a saying that, if Israel could only keep the Law perfectly for one day, the Messiah would come. Obviously to men who held beliefs like that, Jesus was someone who was a sinner and who, worse than that, was doing incalculable harm, for he was delaying the coming of the Kingdom of which they dreamed and for which they prayed and for the hastening of which they lived the most strenuously disciplined life. We must never think that Paul wished to eliminate the very name of Jesus because he was a bad man; it was because he was a good man that he hated Jesus, only he did not rightly understand what goodness was.

When we think of Paul's background, all that he had learned and been taught and had studied, it becomes easy to see that Jesus was the very contradiction of all that, and that Christianity was the complete denial of it. When Paul persecuted as he did, he thought genuinely that he was serving God and that he was hastening the coming of God's Kingdom among men and that he was removing one of the great barriers to the coming of that Kingdom.

A new creature

So then we can see that Paul sincerely thought that he was truly serving God when he sought to obliterate Christianity. We must now try to understand how he came to be the man who could say, "Christ means life to me", and how he, who sought to destroy the very name of Christ, became the man who wore himself out carrying that name to all men he could reach.

The conduct of the persecuted

There were two main streams of influence which played upon Paul until he was ripe and ready for that change. One came from outside him. It was *the conduct of those who were persecuted*. At this time Paul was spending his life dragging Christians into prison, bringing them forcibly to trial, exerting every effort to make them deny the name of Christ and sometimes even exacting the death penalty when they remained steadfast in their faith. Everywhere he saw those Christians meeting trouble and trial with joy; everywhere he saw them meeting argument and even torture with a steadfastness which would not be moved; everywhere he saw them meeting the prospect of death with a serene courage that could not be shaken. Inevitably the thought came to him, "There must be something in this Christianity. Men cannot suffer and die like that for a delusion."

It was not to be the last time in history that the sheer courage of the Christians had its effect upon their persecutors. Much later than this, one of the greatest figures in the Christian Church was a man called Tertullian. In his early days he was a heathen and a Roman lawyer. Often he was involved in the trials of the Christians. He saw these men and women going to death with a laugh or a smile like victors going to a triumph. He said that the Christians conquered in dying; he spoke of the blood of the martyrs being the seed from which the Church grew. He wrote, "The very stubbornness which you are so much irritated by is the very thing that leads men to Christianity. For how can the man who sees it help inquiring whence it comes? And when he has inquired, how can he help accepting the faith the Christians hold?" So Tertullian, the Roman lawyer and prosecutor, saw these Christians face every kind of death, and there came to him the feeling that there must be something which enabled men to die like that; and when he investigated the matter he could not but become a Christian.

Later yet there is a legend which tells how in the days of the great persecutions forty men in a Roman legion were condemned to death because they were Christians. It was midwinter and bitterly cold. The regiment was camped beside a lake that was frozen over, and the commander gave orders that the forty men should be stripped naked and sent out on the lake to march and counter-march until they either recanted or dropped down frozen to death. Meanwhile on the shores of the lake there were set food and clothes and there were lit great fires in an attempt to lure these men from their loyalty to Christ by the offer of food and clothes and warmth if they would only recant. So the forty marched and counter-marched and as they marched they sang a song, "Forty wrestlers, wrestling for Christ." Even the heathen soldiers and officers looked on amazed at their fortitude and courage. Then one gave in; he broke from the ranks and fled to the warmth and the comfort of the fire. The song of the band faltered because they could no no longer sing that they were forty wrestlers wrestling for Christ. The commander of the legion saw it. "Whatever else these men are," he said, "they are gallant souls." And he stripped off his clothes and walked out and marched with them. "It would be an honour," he said, "to die with men like these." Now they were forty again and their song rang out once more; and they marched until they died and the commander with them. The very heroism of the Christians had won him for the faith.

That is the kind of thing that Paul had to watch again and again. He had to watch men dying with gallantry and even joy. Strange doubts were rising in his mind. Must there not be something in this?

We must ever remember that, if we want to win men for Christ, arguments will seldom do it. The only unanswerable argument for Christianity is the argument of a Christian life.

Stephen

But there was one man above all others who affected Paul. That man's name was Stephen. Very early the Church had got into a difficulty. The Jews had always looked after their poor people carefully. Every day there were officials of the synagogue whose duty it was to take a collection, called "The Basket," from those who were well off and to distribute the proceeds among those who were poor and destitute. Naturally the Christian Church took over this custom. But in the Church there were Jews who were natives of Palestine and there were Jews who had come from other lands. There arose a complaint that there was a difference in the treatment of the native Jews and the foreign Jews and that the distribution was made with favouritism. The apostles themselves could not leave off their preaching to deal with this complaint, and they appointed seven men to look after this matter of whom Stephen was one (Acts 6).

But Stephen did much more than that. He became one of the most powerful and effective debaters in the Christian Church. He carried the war right into the enemy's camp. He went into the synagogue and there he set forth and pressed upon the Jews the claims of Christ.

In Jerusalem there was only one Temple but there were as many synagogues and more as there are churches in any of our great cities. A legend says that there were more than 400 synagogues in Jerusalem. Very often Jews who had gone abroad and come back home had their own synagogue in the city. So there would be a synagogue of African Jews and of Roman Jews and of Babylonian Jews.

There was one particular synagogue in which Stephen did a great deal of his debating. It was called the Synagogue of the Freedmen and Cyrenians and Alexandrians and those from Cilicia and Asia (Acts 6:9). We have already seen that Tarsus was the metropolis of Cilicia and that Paul came from Tarsus. He must have sat in that synagogue and listened to Stephen preach and taken part in the debates which he provoked. There is always something about a man who speaks with a burning sincerity, and Paul must have felt that there must be something in this Christianity to make Stephen speak as he did.

Bit by bit another dent was being made in Paul's defences. First there was the calm courage and the heroism of the persecuted Christians; now there was the utter sincerity which shone through Stephen. Paul was far from giving in yet but the whole thing was making him think furiously. At the back of his mind were doubts that could not be stilled.

The death of Stephen

Stephen's career was short. He was arrested and brought to trial. The speech that he made in his own defence is recorded in Acts 7. It was not so much a defence of Christianity as a flaming attack on the hard-heartedness of the Jews. It is difficult for us to understand now but at the back of it were three charges against them. The first was that God's truth was not for Jews only but for everyone. Think how that must have sounded to a people who believed that God had no use for anyone else. The second was that it was not necessary to worship God in the Temple; men could worship him anywhere in all the world, for he did not live in temples made with hands. Think how that that must have sounded to men who believed that the one sacred spot in the world was the Temple in Jerusalem. The third was that in any event a study of their history showed beyond doubt that the Jews had all along consistently resisted, persecuted and killed the messengers of God. Think how that must have sounded to men who thought they were better than any other men in the world. Finally, said Stephen, this resistance to God had culminated in the crucifying of Jesus.

At once Stephen was arrested and tried for blasphemy. The penalty for blasphemy was stoning to death. A man was stripped naked. He was taken up to a height and then thrown down and great boulders were rolled down upon him until finally he was crushed and battered to death. It was one of the most agonising deaths that any man might die.

Paul was there. In fact he was more than a mere spectator; he was taking a leading part in this execution (Acts 7:58). And Paul

saw a demonstration of Christian courage and of Christian fortitude such as he had never seen. As Stephen died this agonising
death his face was not twisted in fear and in pain, but was like
the face of an angel. He did not look with bitterness on those
who were killing him nor was there the least fragment of hatred
in his heart. He prayed, "Lord lay not this sin to their charge",
and so he died.

Augustine once said that the Church owed Paul to the prayer
of Stephen. Once again Paul was left astonished. Could Christianity be a delusion when it enabled a man to face death like that?
Could Christianity be an evil thing when it made a man die with
courage and forgiveness like that? Paul was far from submitting
yet; but thoughts and feelings had been awakened in his heart
that were beginning a secret warfare there.

Paul's own spiritual experience

We said there were two main streams of influence which
played upon Paul. The first came from outside. It was the be-
haviour of the persecuted Christians. The second came from
inside him. *It was his own spiritual experience of the Law.* Paul was a
Rabbi and a Pharisee. We saw that this meant every single act of
his life was regulated by the Law. The Law began with the great
principles of the Ten Commandments, but it went on until there
was some regulation which covered every part and every detail,
every action and every thought in life. Now any man who seeks
to rule his life by Law and Law alone soon discovers certain things.

(i) He discovers that the Law can tell him what to do, but
it cannot give him any help towards doing it. If a man has
studied the Law, he knows exactly what he ought to do; but that
is no guarantee at all that he can do it. A man may know exactly
how to play golf; theoretically he may know how to play every
stroke; but that is not to say he can play it. A man may know
exactly what it means to be good but that is not to say that he can
be good. That is what Paul found. He tells us, "For I do not do
the good I want, but the evil I do not want is what I do"
(Romans 7:19). He said "I can will what is right, but I cannot do
it" (Romans 7:18).

Paul found himself in the position of knowing what he ought to do and wanting to do it and yet being unable to do it. He found himself knowing what he should not do and not wanting to do it and yet not being able to stop himself doing it. Here was an agonising situation, which could drive a man mad. The better the man was, the more agonising the situation was, because the better the man was, the higher the standards he would of necessity set himself. So over and over again Paul must have said to himself, "I have got this holy Law of God; it is the most precious thing in the world; it tells me what I ought to do and I believe it and accept it with my whole heart and I want to do it—*but I can't.*" He had the Law, but he had no power to keep it; the Law could tell him what to do, but could give him no help towards doing it. Paul must have felt that he was doomed to a losing battle all his life.

(ii) But any man will discover something else about the Law. He will discover, if he tries to rule his life by Law and nothing else, that in a completely paradoxical way it is actually the cause of sin. He discovers that, by a curious yet universal quirk in human nature, he is no sooner told not to do a thing than it becomes the very thing he wants to do. In the old story of the Garden of Eden the one fruit Eve wanted to eat was the one she was forbidden to eat. The cow always wants the grass that is just beyond the fence. "Stolen fruits are sweetest." We all know what a fatal fascination the thing that we are forbidden always has.

Paul found that. "If it had not been for the law, I should not have known sin. I should not have known what it is to covet if the law had not said, 'You shall not covet'. " (Romans 7:7). The very fact that we are told not to covet a thing is what makes us want it. So Paul was faced with the heartbreaking situation that the very Law which showed him the way to goodness was what made him want the wrong things. As far as he could see when he faced the thing honestly, life was going to be one long torture between two tensions which tugged in opposite directions.

(iii) But there is still another basic thing about the Law. It is exactly like a leash. In life there are the things we want to do and which we know to be wrong. Law says to us, "Don't do them." It is like a leash to hold us back. But there is always the chance of a leash snapping. Our desires say to us, "Do this." Our will says to us, "You must not do it." But at any moment our desires may prove too strong and our will may prove too weak and so the leash may snap.

Life can never be comfortable when one half of us is struggling against the leash which the other half is holding on to. Life can never be safe when a man does not know just when this leash is going to snap. If all he has to keep him right is Law, then struggle and insecurity must be the permanent marks of his life. And Paul knew that.

The dilemma of Paul

So then we have Paul still hating Christ and the Christians with all his heart; but in that same heart strange feelings are moving. The sight of the calm heroism of the Christians had left him wondering how they could show it. The death of Stephen had left him wondering what was Stephen's secret. His devotion to the Law seemed to be making more and more of a tension and a struggle of life. Whatever else the young Paul was, he was a desperately unhappy man.

D

CHAPTER SIX

The Heavenly Vision

Paul seeks to still his doubts

Outwardly Paul was still the orthodox Jewish Rabbi, fanatically in love with the Law, fanatically opposed to Christianity and to Jesus Christ. But inwardly his mind was a raging battle and an increasing tension. However hard he tried to evade the issue nagging at the back of his mind, the question persisted, "Was it possible that Jesus Christ was right and that he was wrong?"

In this mental situation Paul did what so many people have done. He tried to still his doubts by plunging into a still more furious activity. Let us take a very simple analogy. Perhaps a boy has gone out to play football; he has been told to be home at 8 o'clock. He knows that 8 o'clock has come and that he ought to leave the game and go home. He does not want to go home; and so he plunges into the game with redoubled vigour in order to silence the voice which tells him he ought to stop.

That is precisely what Paul did. He did not want to think; he did not want to face the issue. And so he rushed into still more violent persecution. So far as he could, he had, as he might have put it, cleaned up Jerusalem. But word came that there was a strong community of Christians in Damascus, away in the North.

Damascus was not in Palestine at all; it was in Syria; and before Paul could begin operations there he had to make certain arrangements. The supreme court of the Jews was the Sanhedrin, which had jurisdiction not only over the Jews in Jerusalem and in Palestine, but over every Jew in the world. All over the world there were Jews who had emigrated to foreign lands. Many of them had never seen Jerusalem, because their families had been in these strange places for generations; but wherever a Jew might be the decisions of the Sanhedrin were binding upon him. So Paul had to get authority from the Sanhedrin to go to Damascus and deal with the Christians there.

Here is an interesting point. The Greek word for an envoy is *apostolos*. An *apostolos* was anyone sent out with a delegated authority from some higher power; and, of course, *apostlos* is exactly the same word as the English word *apostle*. When Paul set out to Damascus he was the apostle of the Sanhedrin with the task of wiping out the name of Jesus Christ; when he reached Damascus he was the apostle of Jesus Christ with the task of carrying his name to every land. Within the limits of that journey Paul's life had been turned upside down.

The journey to Damascus

Paul received his authority to persecute and set out for Damascus. Everything in that journey was calculated to bring matters to a head. It was 140 miles from Jerusalem to Damascus. To us that is a short journey, less than, say, from Glasgow to Inverness. With modern methods of transport it could have been covered in considerably less than a day. But for Paul it was a journey that had to be made upon foot; and, even travelling fairly fast, such a journey would take at least a week.

And now comes the salient fact—*that week would be a week of loneliness for Paul.* His travelling companions would be members of the Temple guard. They were roughly the equivalent of police constables detailed to make the necessary arrests in Damascus. Now Paul was a Rabbi and a fanatical Pharisee. For such a man it was not only improper, it was unlawful, that he should hold any kind of communication with ordinary common people who did not observe the ceremonial law as he did. They were there to carry out his orders but certainly not to walk with him, or talk with him, or hold any kind of fellowship with him. The picture of that journey in our mind's eye must be of Paul striding on detached, alone, isolated, aloof, wrapped in thought. For Paul that week's walk to Damascus was a time when he was compelled to think. The thoughts which he had evaded and the issues which he had refused to face and the problems which he had tried to drown in action now rose up and faced him and there was no way round them.

Tolerance or persecution?

In addition to all the thoughts which we saw in the last chapter, there must have been at least two more things in Paul's mind. The first was the memory of Gamaliel. When Paul had come as a student to Jerusalem he had sat at the feet of Gamaliel (Acts 22:3). He was one of the most famous of all the wise men of the Jews. He was one of the four great teachers of the Law to whom the highest title, Rabban, was given. There was a saying that, "From the day when Rabban Gamaliel the Elder died, the glory of the Law ceased and purity and abstinence died." No man was ever held in greater admiration and respect than Gamaliel. And this man had been the master of Paul.

Gamaliel had one outstanding characteristic by which all men knew him, and that was his gracious tolerance. He was very different from the narrow, grimly fanatical, Gentile-hating Rabbis who were so common. He was a man with the widest sympathies and the most gracious personality and the biggest and the gentlest heart. It is precisely thus that he appears in his one entrance on the stage of New Testament action. When Peter and John were arrested and brought before the Sanhedrin, their defence aroused that court to fury, and the consensus of opinion was all in favour of their immediate execution. Then Gamaliel gave his opinion. "Take care what you do with these men," he said. "Let them alone. For if this plan or this undertaking is of men, it will fail; but if it is of God, you will not be able to overthrow them. You might even be found opposing God!" (Acts 5:33–40). There in that scene comes out all the wise tolerance and the gracious gentleness of the man.

We have to compare the tolerant sympathy of Gamaliel with Paul breathing out threatenings and slaughter against the Christians. Surely if Gamaliel was Paul's master, again and again he must have tried to instil some of his own gentleness into this fiery disciple of his; and surely Paul with that blazing heart of his must have been irked and irritated by what he considered the softness of the older man. So in this long, lonely walk Paul's mind must have gone over and over the talks he had had with Gamaliel. He could not but respect Gamaliel, and, now that he had time to think and could not avoid thinking, he must have wondered if Gamaliel was right and he was wrong.

The face of Jesus Christ

It seems to us that there must have been something else as well. Many scholars (perhaps most scholars) would dispute this or even strenuously deny it, but it seems to us that Paul must have seen Jesus in the days of his flesh.

It must have been just at the time when Jesus' ministry in Jerusalem had attracted most attention that Paul was a student there. It is difficult to see how the young Pharisee could have avoided hearing of and actually seeing this Galilaean who was upsetting Jerusalem so much. In 2 Corinthians 2:16 when Paul is stressing the importance of spiritual things as against the things of the flesh he drops the mysterious remark, "From now on, therefore we regard no one from a human point of view; even though we once regarded Christ from a human point of view, we regard him thus no longer." It is difficult to see how that can mean anything other than that Paul had at least seen Jesus in the days of His flesh.

Now Paul's journey from Jerusalem to Damascus could be made in more than one way. But in all likelihood he travelled up the Jordan valley and through Galilee. There was the land of Galilee; there were the towns and the villages and the lake so inextricably connected with the name and the mission of Jesus. Paul was driven to think. He could see again the face of the man he had hated. He could hear again that voice. Again he was confronted with the question, "Could it be that this Jesus was right and I am wrong?"

The heavenly vision

Paul's thoughts much resemble a trapped animal. Just as the trapped animal darts this way and that but finds always that there is no escape, so Paul's thoughts chased round and round and always came back to the same torturing question. Then the crack came.

There is one intensely significant point in the narrative of the vision that came to Paul. *It came at midday* (Acts 26:13). Now every normal traveller rested at midday. Travelling was normally done in the cool of the morning and the cool of the later after-noon and early evening. But during the burning heat of noon the caravan rested. The fact that Paul was pressing on at midday shows that he was driving himself and his companions to the limit of human endurance, so that he could get away from these thoughts of his and find solace in violent action.

They had climbed the slopes of Mount Hermon and were looking down on Damascus. Damascus is said to be the oldest city in the world. It was old two thousand years before Paul, in the days of Abraham, and it is still a great city today nearly two thousand years after Paul's death. It was a lovely city. It was set on the very edge of the desert but the two rivers Abanah and Pharpar made it an oasis of fertile green. In that green plain nestle the whitewashed, flat-roofed houses so that someone once, in a famous phrase, called Damascus "a handful of pearls in a goblet of emerald". But Paul was not thinking of the beauty or of the history of Damascus. All that he was thinking of was getting to grips with the hated Christians.

Then something happened. We know that in that part of the world there frequently come sudden thunderstorms, when the cold air from Mount Hermon meets the hot breath of the desert. But what may well have been to others a sudden crash of thunder and a sudden blaze of lightning was something far more to Paul.

We must remember that this vision came to Paul and to no one else. It was a personal and private message and appearance of the Risen Christ to Paul. At the crash and the blaze Paul fell to earth like a man unconscious. Then he heard a voice speaking to him, not in the Greek that he used among strangers, but in the Hebrew which was his mother tongue. The voice said, "Saul, Saul, why do you keep on persecuting me?" Paul answered, "Who are you, sir?" The voice said, "I am Jesus whom you keep on persecuting. It is so hard for you to keep on kicking against the goads."

When a young ox was yoked to a cart for the first time, he did not like it and quite often tried to kick the cart to pieces with his hind legs. At the front of the cart was fixed a bar with a row of wooden spikes on it and every time the ox tried to kick the cart to pieces he kicked his legs against the spikes and hurt himself. Very soon he learned that it was better far to be obedient to the reins and to the yoke.

Jesus was saying to Paul, "Paul, you are just hurting yourself by all your struggles; you will never know peace until you submit yourself to me." And then Paul surrendered. "Lord," he said, "what do you want me to do?" He turned like a child to Jesus and said, "Whatever you want me to do, I'll do it." Jesus told him to go into Damascus and there he would get his instructions. Then Paul rose from the earth but he could not see and his attendants had to lead him by the hand into Damascus. For three days he lay there blind and unable to eat or drink.

The contrast

Think of the contrast between Paul's plans and what really happened. He had set out from Jerusalem; he had pressed on to Damascus; he had thought of himself entering Damascus like a whirlwind of vengeance to strike terror into the hearts of the Christians. Instead he came into that city a helpless, blind man, led like a child by the hand. But the long struggle was over. Paul had capitulated. He who had been the enemy had become the slave of Christ.

CHAPTER SEVEN

In Perils Oft

A certain disciple at Damascus named Ananias
It was as a blind and helpless man that Paul entered the city of
Damascus. His attendants led him by the hand to the house of a
man called Judas, who lived in the street called Straight. This
was a great street which ran straight as an arrow from the east to
the west side of Damascus. It was divided into three parts. In the
centre was a road on which the chariots and the horsemen and the
wheeled traffic went; and on each side there was a way for the
thronging pedestrians. It is still there to-day; only to-day it is
called "Souk el Tawil" which means the "Long Bazaar"because,
under a sheltering canopy of corrugated iron, it is lined with
little shops and booths where the merchants and the people sell
and buy.

For three days Paul lay there without eating and unable to see.
But he was not to be left that way. There came a message from
God to a certain disciple of Damascus called Ananias which told
him to go to that house, enquire for Paul and lay his hands upon
him so that he might receive his sight again. Paul also received a
message from God that this Ananias would come.

Ananias was shocked at the request. Paul's reputation had gone
before him and the Christians in Damascus knew that the
supreme persecutor had come with the avowed intention of
wiping them out. But God told Ananias that, whatever Paul
might have been before, now he was destined to be one of the
greatest servants of Christ and to bring the message of the gospel
to many people and to many lands.

So Ananias went; and when he entered the room where Paul
was, he said a great thing. His first words were, "Brother Saul."

He knew Paul's history and his reputation; he knew why he had come to Damascus; and yet he called him *brother*.

We know nothing whatever about Ananias except this one incident. But to him belongs the great honour of welcoming Paul into the Christian Church. He might so easily have come to him with suspicion; he could even have come with bitterness for all that he had done; but he came calling him *brother* and so showed him at the very beginning how a Christian could forgive.

Ananias laid his hands upon Paul and he received his sight again. Then Paul was baptised. We generally think of baptism in connection with babies. But in New Testament times grown men and women were being baptised because they were coming from heathen homes which had never heard of Christ or from Jewish homes which were hostile to him. Baptism in these early days was a man confessing his faith and declaring that from that time forward he was a follower of Christ.

Once in Africa there was a missionary who carried out bap tisms in a wonderful way. When an African became a Christian he had to be baptised. The missionary took him down to a shallow river. He took him into the middle of the river and he placed his head for a moment beneath the clean running water; and then he made him come out of the river, not on the side on which he had come in, but on the other side. It was as if to say, "This baptism has cleansed you; this day is a dividing line in your life; from to-day you are a new man."

Paul never forgot the day of his baptism. He would be clothed in white garments; he would be baptised not just by having a few drops of water sprinkled over him but by being completely dipped in the clean water. Afterwards he said that when he was dipped below the water it was just like being buried; and when he emerged from the water it was just like rising from a grave as Jesus had risen from the dead. It was just as if the old Paul who had been the sworn enemy of Jesus had died and a new Paul, who was the pledged servant of Jesus, had risen in his place (Romans 6:4–6).

In the synagogue in Damascus

Then Paul did a very brave thing. Straightway he went to the synagogue in Damascus and witnessed for Christ there. He stood up in front of everyone and told them that he believed this Jesus, whom he had hated, was none other than the Son of God and that from now on he was His servant and His man. The Jews were shocked and infuriated. They looked on Paul as a renegade and a traitor. It would have been so much easier for him to go where no one knew about him and his history and to start his new life from there. But he was determined to show the people who knew him best what a change had come upon him.

Rudyard Kipling has a poem called "Mulholland's Vow." It is about a man whose work was on a cattle boat. His job was to look after the cattle in the great hold between decks. Once there was a terrific storm and the cattle broke loose and they were plunging, mad with fear, about the hold. Mulholland might have been killed by their horns and their hooves at any moment. In his danger he made a bargain with God. He said that if God would save him from this he would stop his hard-drinking, hard-swearing way of life and become a preacher. In an almost miraculous way Mulholland escaped death and the ship came to harbour. So he decided he would keep his part of the bargain and become a preacher; only he decided that he would get as far away from the cattle-boats as he could and that he would preach God's name, as he said himself, "handsome and out of the wet." But God's word came to him, "Back you go to the cattle-boats and preach my gospel *there*."

He wanted to take the easy way and to go away and preach where no one knew him; God ordered him back to the people who knew him best and who knew what he had been—and Mulholland went. That is what Paul did. He was a changed man and he was not afraid to show it in Damascus. The Jews would hate him because he who had been their champion was now their opponent; the Christians would regard him with grave suspicion because he had done them so much harm. It did not matter to Paul. With that supreme courage of his, it was in the synagogue at Damascus that first he spoke for Christ.

Away to Arabia

But so many things had happened that Paul was left breathless and bewildered. He knew that he must have time to think things out and to decide just what he was going to do; and for that he had to be alone. So he left Damascus and went away to the deserts of Arabia to be absolutely alone with the sand and the sun and the stars.

Some scholars think that he may have gone away to Mount Sinai. It was there that Moses had received the Ten Commandments from God; and it would be very fitting that Paul should there receive his commission to preach the gospel of Jesus Christ. If he was there for long—we do not know how long he stayed alone—he would be able to make a living at his trade. Doubtless the wandering Arabs would be glad to give him food and drink for repairing their tents.

It is interesting to note how great men have invariably gone away to be alone before starting on their life work. Francis of Assisi was one. They used to call him the man who loved mountains, because whenever he had some great decisions to make he would go away to a mountain top to think things out and to listen to the voice of God. Jesus did that. He began his ministry by going away into the desert and deciding in face of his temptations what he was going to do.

If ever we have a problem to solve, if ever we do not know just what course to follow, we must try to be alone and to do two things. First, we must try to think this through for ourselves; and second, we must ask God what he wants us to do and listen for his commands.

Back to Damascus

Once he had thought things out and knew what God wanted him to do, Paul went straight back to Damascus. He spent a long time there, perhaps as long as three years; and all the time he was in the synagogue and on the streets preaching the gospel of Jesus.

Soon there began that series of hairbreadth escapes of which Paul's life was full. The Jews became angrier and angrier. Remember that Paul was a trained Rabbi and had spent years reading and studying the Old Testament. His training made him a first-class debater and, when the Jews could not match his argument with argument, they determined to match it with force. Paul's influence was tremendous. The very fact that this man who had been the prince of persecutors had been changed so radically made people believe that there must be something in Christianity. Even those who could not follow his argument of words were moved by the argument of his life. The Jews could stand it no longer. They determined that he must be killed.

They knew he was planning a visit to Jerusalem and night and day their hired assassins lurked at the gates of Damascus ready to murder him when he came out. Paul had to escape in secrecy. The walls of ancient cities were very thick, so thick that often carriage and pair could be driven along their top. Sometimes houses were built on the top of the wall and sometimes they had windows or little balconies jutting out beyond the wall. Paul had a friend who lived in one of these houses. So the Christians took him and, in the darkness of the night, let him down in a basket over the wall; and he escaped away in safety. So here is the beginning. Paul had begun not only his preaching but his adventuring for Christ.

To Jerusalem

By this time Paul had been a Christian for about three years. So far as we know, as yet he had never met any of the leaders of the Christian Church. Life was much more self-contained in those days. True, Jerusalem was only about 140 miles from Damascus; but at that time there were no newspapers, no radio or television, no speedy travel and the people in Jerusalem would hear only vague stories and travellers' tales of what was happening away in Damascus. So Paul decided to set out for Jerusalem and to meet the leaders of the Church there.

But when he arrived he found the atmosphere anything but friendly. The last time he had been in Jerusalem he had been dragging men and women to prison and even to death. He had been breathing threats and murder against the Christians (Acts 9:1); he was the hammer and the scourge of the Christian

Church. The Christians of Jerusalem found it frankly incredible that the Paul they had known and dreaded had been changed into a man who was now as passionately in love with Christ as he had passionately hated Him.

There was one man, however, with a big and gracious heart and a tremendous belief that God could work miracles with human nature. His name was Barnabas. Originally he had been called Joseph. He was a Levite. Now the Levites had a very comfortable life. They were the people who looked after the work of the Temple. The priests looked after the sacrifices and the services but the Levites looked after all the material arrangements and the music. In return for this they got a share of the Temple sacrifices and they lived practically free of charge.

Barnabas gave up all this for the sake of Christ. He came from Cyprus where he had some property and was a wealthy man. But he sold all and gave the proceeds to the Christian Church to help the poor and the needy. He literally gave up everything, his money, his estate, his prestige, his comfort for the sake of Christianity. He must have been a kindly and a gracious soul because his name Barnabas means "son of exhortation," or "son of consolation." He was the kind of man that anyone might go to in trouble. Not only was he kind but he was a tall, handsome, impressive figure who commanded people's respect whenever they saw him.

This gracious, universally respected Barnabas saw Paul regarded with suspicion and kept at a distance and his warm heart could not bear it. He took him by the hand and led him into the Christian assembly. It was as if he said, "You know me; and you know that I would never do anything to hurt the Church. I stand sponsor for this man Paul; I will be his guarantor; from this day forward he is my friend." Immediately Paul was accepted by everyone. At the moment there were only two great men of the Church in Jerusalem, James the brother of Jesus and Peter himself. And Paul spent the happiest two weeks with Peter. We can well believe that Peter told Paul all kinds of stories about Jesus and all kinds of things that Jesus had said so that Paul knew Jesus better than ever when that precious fortnight had passed.

In peril again

Then again the almost defiant courage of Paul emerged. He had come to Jerusalem not only to learn but to witness for Christ. Into those very synagogues where once he had debated with Stephen, among those very people who had known him as a persecutor, he went and preached the gospel and argued the claims of Christ. Once again the Jews could not stand it. They could not silence him in debate and they determined to silence him by death.

Once again Paul had to flee for his life. This time the Christians managed to smuggle him out of the city down to Caesarea on the sea-coast and from there he caught ship to Tarsus. He had been a follower of Christ for only three years and in those three years twice the Jews had tried to assassinate him and twice he had escaped death by a hair's breadth.

These attacks on his life were actually compliments to Paul. They showed how dangerous the Jews considered him to be. People never persecute and seek to kill a man who is of no importance. By trying to kill him the Jews showed that they were desperately afraid of the victories he might yet win for Christ.

In Syria and Cilicia

So Paul escaped from Jerusalem and came to Tarsus and to Syria and Cilicia. That was his native place. And now for nine years he disappears from history. No doubt he had gone back to his own folk and his own town that he might try to win for Christ those whom he knew best and those who knew him best. And no doubt all the time he was thinking and studying and working, preparing himself, although he did not know it, for the great task of evangelising the Gentiles which was to come to him.

CHAPTER EIGHT

First in Antioch

Antioch

Though Paul had vanished from history in Cilicia the sequence of events was still working itself out. Away up in the very north of the province of Syria there was a city called Antioch. It stood near the coast, fifteen miles from the place where the River Orontes poured its waters into the Mediterranean Sea. Antioch was not a very old city as cities go and had been founded about three hundred years before Jesus came into the world by one of the successors of Alexander the Great. But in the time of Paul, Antioch, with a population of almost a quarter of a million, was the third greatest city in the world. Only Rome and Alexandria surpassed it.

Antioch was a lovely city. Right through it for a length of five and a half miles ran a famous street, paved with white marble for half its length. There was a central road along which the traffic passed and on each side a broad path for the pedestrians and for the shops. These side paths for much of their length were roofed over into porticos and colonnades which gave the people shelter from the sun and from the rain. Right round Antioch there was a vast wall which followed the contours of the hills and the valleys until it looked as if the hills and the valleys themselves were standing sentinel and guard over it. Antioch was so near the sea that the sea breezes reached the city and tempered the heat so that it had one of the finest climates in the world.

Antioch was a cosmopolitan city. A Greek writer said that all one had to do was to sit in the market place of Antioch and one would see the men and customs of all the world. Within its walls there were four main kinds of people. There were the native Syrians who were the original inhabitants of the country. There were the Greeks who had been the original founders of the city. There were the Romans who were now the rulers of the world. There were the Jews who had their own governing council and who were allowed to live their own way of life.

Antioch was a wicked city, and was a by-word for luxurious living. Day and night alike the citizens went on with their feasting and their licentious ways. It was a city which was famous for all kinds of sport. Especially famous were the races for chariots. All the city was divided into two factions, the Blues and the Greens; the rivalry was like that between Celtic and Rangers in Scotland; even Roman Emperors had been known to wear the colours of the rival teams. But in particular Antioch was famous for the worship of Daphne. There was an old Greek legend which told how Apollo fell in love with a mortal maid called Daphne. He pursued her and was about to catch her when she was changed into a daphne bush. That, the Greeks thought, was where the daphne bush had its origin and got its name. Five miles out of the town of Antioch were the groves of the temple of Daphne. To the temple were attached scores of priestesses who were nothing other than sacred prostitutes. The old story was re-enacted in the temple groves. The worshippers pursued the priestesses through the laurel groves and caught them and the "morals of Daphne" was a phrase which was proverbial in the ancient world for loose living. So immoral a city was Antioch that in later days a famous Roman general put it out of bounds for his troops on leave.

Antioch had a gift for sarcastic speech and for fixing nicknames to people. Years after this there came to Antioch the Emperor Julian. He was a man who wanted to go back to the old ways. He wore a long beard as the ancient philosophers used to do and the Antiochenes nicknamed him "the Goat" and shouted to him to go "and weave it into ropes." He wanted to bring back the old sacrifices of animals and the Antiochenes nicknamed him "the Butcher." The people of Antioch were a lighthearted and ribald lot who showed respect for no one.

Two great happenings in Antioch

In that great, wicked, cosmopolitan city of Antioch two great things happened. When persecution had been going on in Jerusalem, some of the Christians had decided that they must leave their native place and go where they could worship God in peace. Some of them found their way to Antioch.

Up to this time nearly all the Christians had been Jews. We have seen how the Jews thought themselves the chosen people and that God had absolutely no use for any other race or any other nation. At first the Christians were the same. They thought that Christianity was only for the Jews; it never struck them that it was for all the earth. They did not dream of sharing their new joy and their new privilege and their new knowledge of God with other people.

But something happened in Antioch. Maybe the Christians who fled there were so full of the happiness of the gospel that they felt that they had to share it with everyone they met. Whatever happened, in Antioch, for the first time, Christians began to preach the gospel to Gentiles. In Antioch for the first time they glimpsed the truth that Christianity was for all the world and that Jesus had come not to be the Jewish Messiah only but to be the Saviour of all men everywhere. So these Christians who had fled to Antioch began to preach the gospel not only to fellow Jews but to anyone who would listen to them. Had it not been for them we might never have been Christians to-day.

The other great thing which happened at Antioch was that there the followers of Jesus were first called Christians. Without doubt this was one of those nicknames which the Antiochenes were so quick to find. The Jews did not invent the name for they called the Christians Nazarenes, after Jesus of Nazareth. The Christians did not invent that name, for they called themselves "the brethren" or "the saints." It must have been some citizen of Antioch who first half-contemptuously coined this nickname— those Christfolk, those Christians—and it stuck. It was a name given in contemptuous jest but it became the most famous name in the world.

E

A new leader is sought and found

The headquarters of the new Church were still in Jerusalem and when word went back there that up in Antioch the gospel was being preached to the Gentiles, the leaders of the Church did not know quite what to make of it. They were Jews and so far it had not struck them that they had a duty to anyone other than their fellow-Jews. So they decided to send an envoy to investigate the matter.

They sent Barnabas and they could not possibly have picked a better man to send. If they had sent some narrow, fanatical Jew, he might well have come back and said that this was all wrong, that a stop must be put to it at once and that this precious privilege must not be shared with the hated Gentiles. But Barnabas was the man with the big heart. To him it was a matter of great rejoicing that so many were being added to the fellowship of the Christian Church.

Barnabas, however, saw one thing quite clearly—that this new enterprise needed a leader; and one with quite special qualifications. It needed a leader who could understand the Jewish point of view, because Jesus himself had been a Jew and the Church had sprung from Judaism; and it needed a leader who could understand the Gentile point of view, who could speak Greek fluently, who would be at home with men of every land. One man flashed into Barnabas's mind and that man was Paul.

Paul was by birth a Jew. Barnabas knew how he could deal with Jews because he had seen him in action in Jerusalem. Paul had been brought up in Tarsus in Cilicia; so he knew all about the life and circumstances and atmosphere of Greek cities. Paul was a Roman citizen and so could go anywhere in all the world. He was the man for this situation. So off to Tarsus went Barnabas to look for him. When he found him he offered him this great job of overseeing the work among the Gentiles. Paul seized the chance with both hands and for a year he worked in Antioch with great success.

The way was opening out. Paul was standing at the very threshold now of his great life-work—that of being the apostle to the Gentiles.

CHAPTER NINE

The Work Whereunto I Have Called Them

The people who administered the Church

When we are thinking and reading about the work of the early Church we will come across again and again certain officials. It will make things easier to understand if we know the names of these officials and what each class of official had to do. There were two main kinds, those who were settled in one place, and those whose work extended all over the Church.

We begin with the second kind because they must have been the real leaders of the Church. First, and most important, were those who were called *Apostles*. The word apostle literally means "one who is sent out." An apostle was like an ambassador who was equipped with all the power of the person who sent him.

When we think of the word apostle we always think of the twelve men whom Jesus specially chose and sent out to carry on His work. But in the early Church the apostles included more than the Twelve. The basic qualification of an apostle was that he must have seen Jesus in the flesh and above all must have been a witness of the Resurrection (Acts 1:21, 22). So we find numbered amongst the apostles Matthias, who was chosen by lot to replace Judas the traitor; James the brother of Jesus (1 Corinthians 15:7); Barnabas (Acts 14:14); Andronicus and Junias (Romans 16:7); Silvanus (1 Thessalonians 2:6); and, of course, Paul himself.

The apostles were exceedingly important people. In those days there was no such thing as a printed book. All books had to be hand-written. That made them very difficult and expensive to produce. A book the size of our New Testament would have cost well over £200 to buy. So when Jesus wanted to leave a record of what He had come to say He could not write a book; He had to write His message upon men. The apostles were those on whom He had written His message, the living epistles of Christ. In the early Church they were the most important of all men because they brought and guaranteed as true the message of Jesus Christ.

Second of those who had no settled sphere of work were the *Prophets*. The prophets were the men who lived very close to God. Long ago Amos had said that God would not do anything but He would reveal it first to His prophets (Amos 3:7). They were the men who gave their lives to prayer, God and then brought God's commands to men. In the early Church they had no houses and no possessions. They usually wandered from place to place thinking of nothing but God's will for men and his message to them.

Now we look at the officials in the early Church whose work was centred in one place. First, there were the *Elders*. Long before Christianity and the Christian Church came into being the Jews had men called elders. Originally, they were just wise old men, who had long experience of life and were able to give wise judgments on difficult questions. In the Christian Church they were just the same. They were the ablest men in the congregation and it was their duty to look after its spiritual affairs and to see that it walked in the right way. Sometimes in the New Testament these elders are also called *Bishops*. The word bishop means simply an "overseer". The elders and the bishops were exactly the same people and "bishop" describes the kind of work the elders did, which was to oversee the Christian community.

Besides the elders there were the *Deacons*. They were usually younger men and their duties were much more practical. They had to see to the financial obligations of the Church and to the care of the poor and the sick and the aged.

In addition to these elders and deacons every Christian community had its *Teachers*. Remember that in the early days books were very scarce; and remember that in those days there was no such thing as the New Testament. It was years later that the Gospels were written. The duty of the teachers was to know all that Jesus did and said; to remember it without mistakes or alterations; and to explain what it meant to those entering the Church for the first time. They were very important because it was into their hands and memories that there was entrusted the Christian message before it was set down in writing.

So in the Christian Church in the time of Paul there were apostles and prophets whose work and whose authority extended all over it; and, within each congregation, there were elders and deacons who looked after its spiritual and the material affairs and teachers who expounded to others the story of Jesus.

Paul's second visit to Jerusalem

For a year Paul worked in Antioch with good success. Then one day there came to Antioch certain prophets from Jerusalem. One of them called Agabus stood up in the congregation and told them that very soon a great famine was going to come upon the East. Immediately the thoughts of the people of Antioch turned towards the Christians at Jerusalem. Jerusalem was the very centre of the Jewish religion and there the Christian Church had a specially hard time. It was a poor Church financially and, if famine came, things would be particularly difficult for them. So the Church at Antioch decided that they would do everything in their power to help the poor Christians at Jerusalem. They did exactly what the Church would do today. Sunday by Sunday as they worshipped, they took a collection which was earmarked to be sent to Jerusalem for the help of the Church there; and when they had collected enough, they gave it to Paul and Barnabas to deliver.

The significance of gift of Antioch

The fact that the Church at Antioch sent this gift to the Church at Jerusalem is very important because it illustrates two things which the Church realised from its earliest days.

(*a*) *It realised that help must be practical.* If people were in trouble it was not enough just to feel sorry for them, or to send kind messages and good advice, or even to pray for them. It was necessary to *do* something to help.

Once there was a wealthy farmer who lived in a country where there was a famine. He used to conduct family prayers in his house every day and used to pray that God would help the poor people who had not enough to eat. One day after prayers his young son said to him, "Father, I wish I had some of your corn." "Why do you wish that?" said the farmer. "Because," said the son, "if I had, I would answer your prayers." The boy was quite right. The farmer prayed to God to help the starving people and he could well have helped them himself.

We must always remember that if people are in trouble and want, our first duty is not just to feel sorry for them but to *do* something for them.

(*b*) *It realised from the first the oneness of the Church*. The people at Antioch did not just live in their own little circle and never think of anyone else. Jerusalem was a long way away but they knew that they were responsible for what was happening not only in Antioch but there also.

We, too, should think of the Church as one great family and never of our own congregation as *The* Church. Our congregation is only one of the many, many units which make up The Church. If one member of a family is in trouble, it is the natural and the proper thing for the other members to help. It should be so with the Church. If we ask, "Why do we make offerings for people in other churches and in other countries?" the answer is that all Christian people are members of the family of Jesus and therefore responsible for helping one another.

The vision in Jerusalem

When Paul was in Jerusalem with this gift, something happened that made still clearer to him the task that God was preparing for him. Years after this, when he was defending himself against the Jews, he told men about it (Acts 22:17–21). He could never be long in any place without preaching the gospel and when he was on this visit he began to preach in Jerusalem.

Always remember that Paul was a Jew and proud of his

lineage. His one passion was to see his fellow countrymen accept Christ and his one grief that they were throwing away all their privileges by their enmity to the gospel. His preaching in Jerusalem met with little or no success. In his disappointment and his grief he went into the Temple to pray and there God sent him a vision. He said to him, "You have been preaching to the Jews; they have refused to listen to you; and they will go on refusing. Leave them alone. Leave Jerusalem, because I am going to send you into distant lands to preach to other nations."

This was a turning point in Paul's life. He had been brought up in the strictest sect of the Pharisees. There had been a time when he had looked on every other nation than the Jews as despised and even hated by God. There had been a time when he had looked not for the salvation but for the destruction of the other nations and the other peoples. Events in Antioch had made him begin to glimpse the truth that the Good News of Jesus was for all men. But now he was brought face to face with a moment of decision. Once and for all he had to cast off all his old convictions and prejudices. He did not yet know how that was to be done but when he went back to Antioch the way suddenly and unexpectedly opened up.

CHAPTER TEN

Sent Forth by the Holy Ghost

The return to Antioch and the commission to the Gentiles

From Jerusalem Paul returned to Antioch with his mind full of the vision which God had sent him and the task that now he knew God had given him to do. That task opened out to him far sooner than he could have expected. In the Church at Antioch there were certain prophets and teachers, Barnabas and Simeon, Lucius and Manaen. This company of deeply devoted men were gathered together and the Spirit of God said to them, "Set apart for me Barnabas and Saul for the work to which I have called them" (Acts 13:1, 2).

The Church at Antioch had taken one of the greatest and most epoch-making steps the Church ever took. Up to this time there had been a certain accidental quality in the spread of Christianity. It is true that at Antioch the gospel had been preached to the Gentiles; but when we read the story we see that it could well have been done simply as an isolated outburst of sudden enthusiasm. But the Church at Antioch set its foot upon a path that was to lead to the ends of the earth. Its leaders were convinced that the preaching to the Gentiles must not be simply an outburst of sudden enthusiasm, a passing exuberance; they were convinced that they must take steps to win the world for Christ. Paul must indeed have seen the hand of God in this. In Jerusalem he had had a vision which told him of his task. At the moment he had not been able to see how that task was to be carried out, but now it was handed to him by the authority of the Church and under the guidance of the Spirit.

To Cyprus

So Paul and Barnabas set out. Antioch was fifteen miles up the River Orontes. At the mouth of the Orontes stood the seaport of Seleuceia looking westward over the Mediterranean Sea; and from the harbour on a clear day you could see the dim outline of the island of Cyprus seventy miles away across the blue waters of the sea.

It was to Cyprus they first turned their steps. No doubt there were many reasons for that choice. For one thing Christianity had already spread to Cyprus and the Christians there were afire with the passion to win all men (Acts 11:20). For another thing, there were many Jews in Cyprus already, for it was a great centre of trade and the Jews were ever traders. Therefore in Cyprus the missionaries would find synagogues which they could use as the initial points of the proclamation of their message. But above all, Barnabas was a native of Cyprus; and Barnabas, with his large warm heart, was precisely the kind of man who would wish first and foremost to take the best news in all the world to his own country and to the people amongst whom he had been brought up.

Cyprus is a large island. It has a coastline measuring no less than 390 miles; and from tip to tip from west to east it measures 190 miles. It was rich and prosperous. Long ago this one island had contained no fewer than nine kingdoms and even in days later than Paul it had no fewer than fifteen considerable cities within its boundaries. It was a great shipbuilding centre where the ships that plied their trade through the Mediterranean Sea were built from the trees of the forests growing in the centre of the island. It was a famous copper-mining centre, producing copper for the craftsman and sulphate of copper for the doctor. It had a flourishing salt industry. The Greeks always described Cyprus by the adjective *Makaria*, which means the happy or the blessed one. And the Greeks used to say that the climate and the fertility of Cyprus were such that its citizens needed to go beyond their own island for nothing; everything they needed for a full and a comfortable life was there. It was a land of vineyards, of corn-fields and of orchards, and of flourishing industries and trades.

To that island Barnabas and Paul set sail. With them they had a young man, John Mark, who also was to become famous. He was the nephew of Barnabas and he was to be what the Authorised Version calls their "minister" (Acts 13:5). That is to say, he was to be their secretary, their courier, their attendant. He was to give assistance with the practical work and problems of the journey.

They landed in Salamis and preached in the synagogue. There they had neither success nor failure to recount. Right across the island they journeyed until they came to Paphos at the other side. Paphos was famous for the worship of the Greek goddess Aphrodite, the goddess of love. At certain seasons of the year there were festivals of the most immoral kind in her honour and Paphos with its background of Aphrodite worship was no easy place in which to preach.

But Paphos was also famous because it was at that time the seat of the Roman governor in Cyprus. His name was Sergius Paulus, a man of wise and enquiring mind. He heard that there had come to his city two men with a new message and a new religion and he summoned them to his residence to hear them expound it.

Sergius Paulus had at his court a Jew called Bar-Jesus. "Bar" is the Hebrew for "son of." So this man was the son of Jesus (or of Joshua for these are both the same name). He was also called Elymas which seems to mean "the wise one." He was an astrologer. In those days astrology had a tremendous grip. Even the wisest and the best of people believed that the lives of men were settled by the motions of the stars. Everyone would like to peer into the future and to know what is going to happen to him. These astrologers claimed to be able to foretell the future by studying the stars. To this day, of course, people dabble in astrology and newspapers pander to superstition by running columns of astrology predictions. Most of the great families and the great men in the time of Paul had their private astrologers and astrology was what we might call a most flourishing ramp.

Elymas saw at once that, if Paul and Barnabas succeeded in winning Sergius Paulus for Christ, his days of influence were finished and he opposed them with all his might. "You mass of deceit and villainy!" Paul said. "You son of the devil!" (That was a pun upon his name—so far from being "Son of Jesus" he was "Son of the devil"). "You enemy of all righteousness; will you not stop making crooked the straight paths of the Lord?" Then he told Elymas that he would be blind for a period and immediately blindness came upon him. We need not for a moment doubt that that happened. The blazing personality of Paul struck terror into the heart of Elymas. We have it on record that once Edward the First of England looked with such blazing rage on one of his courtiers that the man dropped dead from sheer fright.

When the governor saw what had happened and heard the message of Paul, he was convinced of the truth of Christianity and he believed. So the visit to Cyprus had won a Roman governor for Christ.

Saul becomes Paul the leader

When we read the story of the beginning of this journey of Paul and Barnabas in Acts 13:1-13 we notice two things.

(*a*) It was from this time that Paul became the accepted leader of the expedition. At the beginning it is the name of Barnabas that comes first. "Set apart for me Barnabas and Saul for the work." But now the expedition becomes "Paul and his company." It was natural that at first Barnabas should be thought of as the leader; for he was an apostle long before Paul and he was known, respected and famous throughout all the Church, whereas Paul was little known and, where he was known, he was often still suspected. Now by sheer force of personality Paul emerged as the unquestioned leader. It is just here that the beauty of Barnabas's character comes out. He makes no complaint; he knows no jealousy. He recognises the dynamic leadership of Paul and is content to take the second place.

(*b*) Up to Acts 13:13 Paul is consistently called Saul; from this point onwards he becomes Paul. In those days nearly all Jews had two names. One was the Jewish name; one was the Greek name. By their Jewish name they were known amongst their own people and in their own homes; by their Greek name they were known out in the world of business and of trade. Quite often the two names meant the same. For instance Peter is the Greek and Cephas is the Hebrew for a rock; Didymus is the Greek and Thomas is the Hebrew for a twin. Sometimes the only connection between the two names is that they sound alike. For instance a Jew called Eliakim becomes Alcimus in Greek; and the Hebrew Joshua becomes the Greek name Jesus.

It is interesting to ask where Saul the Jew got his Greek name Paul. Many interesting suggestions have been made. Augustine suggested that Paul took the name deliberately because Paulus means "the little fellow," and Paul thought of himself in humility as the least of the apostles, just a little one in the Christian Church. Jerome had a still more interesting theory. It was the custom for great Roman generals to take the name of the country where they won their greatest victories as an additional name. For instance, Scipio won his greatest victories in Africa and he took as his name Scipio Africanus. Our great soldiers still do that. For instance, General Montgomery became Viscount Montgomery of El Alamein. So Jerome suggested that because Paul won Sergius Paulus for Christ he took the name Paulus in commemoration. Others have made the suggestion that the name was a nickname. We have seen that Paul was a small man and the name Paulus could be a nickname meaning, as we might say, "the wee chap." It is much more likely that he always had the name Paul. Maybe his family took that name when they became Roman citizens because the Roman who gave them their citizenship had it. Maybe Paul took the name because it sounded like Saul; he could hardly have called himself Saulus, because in Greek *saulos* means one who waddles along with an almost deformed walk.

However he got it, from this moment he drops the name Saul and becomes Paul. The significance is clear. He had dropped his Jewish name and taken his Gentile name because from now on he was going to devote his life to the winning of the Gentiles.

In Pamphylia

After their tour of Cyprus, Paul and Barnabas and Mark set out again for the mainland. They caught a ship which took them to Perga in Pamphylia. But they did not preach there. Two things happened which were in one sense disasters.

The first is a deduction but the evidence on which the guess is made is good. Pamphylia was a populous district and we are bound to ask why Paul did not preach there. What he did was to go off inland to the province of Galatia and work there. Later when writing to the people of Galatia he said, "You know it was because of a bodily ailment that I preached the gospel to you at first" (Galatians 4:13). When Paul arrived in Galatia he was a sick man.

Here, then, is our explanation. Pamphylia was a low crescent-shaped stretch of land lying between the mountain plateau and the Mediterranean Sea. It was an unhealthy place and notorious for malaria fever. It was there that the agonising malaria with its prostrating headache, his thorn in the flesh, first came upon Paul. That is why he had to leave it so speedily and move on without preaching.

See here the courage and the sheer pertinacity of Paul. It would have been so easy and so natural for him to say to himself, "I am a sick man, I'll quit and go back to Antioch and rest." But Paul pressed on. Once David Livingstone was asked by the London Missionary Society if he was prepared to go to a certain country as a missionary. His answer was, "I am prepared to go anywhere —*so long as it is forward.*" Paul was like that. Backwards he would not go. Pain or no pain, he was for pressing on.

But the second disaster was that there was someone with them who did not feel like that. That someone was John Mark, who left them and went home. The first disaster left Paul with a pain-wracked body; the second left him with a sore heart.

There are many possible explanations of why Mark went home. It may be that, because he was after all just a boy, the first thrilling novelty of the journey had worn off and that he was simply tired of the whole thing. It may be that he disapproved. Mark's home was in Jerusalem and Jerusalem, the centre of Judaism, would be the last place to accept this mission to the Gentiles, which seemed to rob the Jews of their specially privileged place in the economy of God. It may be that Mark was what we would call "soft." It looks as if his father was dead and he had been brought up by his mother (Acts 12:12). In fact, one of the old commentators remarked that Mark went home because he wanted his mother.

Much more likely is the supposition that Mark went home because he did not feel able to face what lay ahead. Paul was a sick man. He had to get out of Pamphylia. One way out was back to Antioch but he rejected that. The other way out was forward. Now that road forward led up precipitous roads to the inland plateau. These roads were hard, none harder in the world. They were cut by mountain streams. Often the beds would be dry; then there would come a deluge of rain, the dry bed would become a raging torrent and the unwary traveller might well be swept to death before he knew what was happening. Worst of all, these roads were the paradise of brigands, marauders who would murder a man for a copper coin. The wonder is not so much that Mark went back as that Paul went on. We should not blame Mark too much, but rather admire the courage of Paul which drove his frail body on to satisfy the imperious urging of his adventurous spirit.

Antioch in Pisidia

So back went Mark, but on went Paul and Barnabas and in due time came to the town of Antioch in Pisidia. There were many Antiochs scattered about Asia Minor for there had been more than one king called Antiocheius and the cities were named in honour of that royal name. This Antioch was designated Antioch in Pisidia or Pisidian Antioch to distinguish it from the others.

Originally Antioch was a Greek city. It had been founded by one of Alexander the Great's successors away back about 300 B.C. It was a very mixed city. In it were the descendants of the original Greek citizens and they must have been adventurous souls to come and stay in a place like that. Besides them were the native Phrygians, a highly emotional and highly unstable race. There were also large numbers of Jews. When the city had first been founded the Jews had been given rights as citizens and they had flocked in to play their parts of the world's traders and the world's bankers. Then in 6 B.C. Antioch became a Roman Colony when Augustus settled there as citizens the veterans of one of his most famous legions so that in that border town they might keep the peace. There would be no lack of variety in any congregation in Antioch. It was in the synagogue that Paul began to preach and the summary of what he said is one of the most interesting Christian documents in the whole New Testament for it is one of the very few records that we have of the preaching of Paul.

CHAPTER ELEVEN

A Word of Exhortation

In the synagogue at Antioch in Pisidia

As he always did, Paul began his mission in Antioch in the synagogue. We have already seen that the synagogue service was peculiarly fitted to give the early Christian missionaries their chance. It had three main parts. First, it had a worship part composed of prayers. Second, it had a part composed of the reading of the Law and the Prophets. Third, there came the address. Here emerged the golden opportunity. There was no one fixed person to give the address as in our churches. Any distinguished visitor might be invited by the ruler of the synagogue to speak. That is what happened in Antioch. Paul and Barnabas can have wasted no time. Right from the moment of their arrival in Antioch they must have made it clear that they were men with a message. So when the Sabbath came and the ruler of the synagogue saw them in their places he immediately said to them, "Brethren, if you have any word of exhortation for the people, say it." Acts gives us a summary of the sermon that Paul preached (Acts 13:16–41). Since it is one of the first of all Christian sermons let us look at it in detail to see the message that Paul brought to the men of his day and the method of appeal that he used. It falls into six main sections.

The culmination of history

It begins in verses 16–23 with a summary of the history of Israel and an insistence that it culminated in the coming of Jesus. It is Paul's conviction that all history is unfolding under the plan of God. Here is something we would do well to take hold of.

Often we are reminded of the sheer length of time. We are told that if we were to take Cleopatra's needle and stick a postage stamp on the top, the height of the monument plus the postage stamp would represent the amount of time there has been since the world began; but the thickness of the postage stamp would represent all the time that has passed since man came into the world. Then we are told that if you go on sticking postage stamps one on the top of the other until you have an edifice the height of Mount Blanc, that height would represent the probable length of time the world will still last.

But the New Testament and the Christian faith are concerned not with the length of time but with the plan of time; not with the insignificance of man but with the vast importance of man in the sight of God. We are to think not of a terrific length of time unwinding itself like some mazily meandering river; but of it driving straight onwards like a Roman road to the goal of the coming of Christ.

Sometimes modern thought urges us to think of the sheer senselessness of history. Lucretius, one of the great Roman thinkers, insisted that there was no sense in anything and that everything was due to the merest chance. A modern thinker said, "History is the record of the follies and the mistakes of men." Such voices invite us to think of history as a disorderly, knotless thread. But the Christian view is that history is planned; not senseless but the result of the wisdom of God.

The witness of John

Verses 24 and 25 relate how Paul reminded that congregation that John the Baptist had borne witness to the fact that Jesus was God's anointed King. Now John, although he had been a man of the wilderness baptising in the River Jordan, had become widely known. Later on in far off Ephesus, Paul found people who were still disciples of John (Acts 19:1–7). So what Paul is saying is, "The best of your own nation, the last of your prophets, bore witness to the greatness of Jesus of Nazareth."

Here again we have something that we must remember. Simple people have found a friend in Jesus; but the greatest men in the world also have bowed before Him. Napoleon once remarked,

F

"I know men and Jesus Christ was more than a man." Sir James Simpson the discoverer of chloroform was once asked, "What do you count as your greatest discovery?" Simpson answered, "My greatest discovery was that Jesus Christ is my Saviour." We need never be ashamed to show our allegiance to Jesus Christ in any company. The greatest men in the world have bowed in humble reverence before him.

The greatest crime in history

In verses 26–29 Paul tells how the Jews crucified Jesus. To make it worse, they had read Sabbath after Sabbath in their synagogues the words of the prophets which told them of the king to come. They should have been ready to welcome him and to crown him and instead they crucified him. All through the New Testament we find that the crucifixion of Jesus is regarded as the greatest and the most shocking crime in history.

It has been said that one of our greatest safeguards against sin lies in our being shocked by it. Perhaps we have read and heard the story of the death of Jesus so often that it passes over our heads and leaves us unmoved.

Florence Barclay, the famous novelist, tells how she heard it for the first time. She was taken to a Good Friday service in an Anglican church. The scripture lesson was being read and it was well read and, child though she was, the thrill of the story caught her. She heard Judas betray Jesus and Peter deny him. She saw Jesus before the Sanhedrin; she saw him before Pilate; she saw him being mocked and scourged and crowned with the crown of thorns. And then came the words: "Then he handed him over to them to be crucified. So they took Jesus, and he went out, bearing his own cross, to the place, called the place of a skull, which is called in Hebrew Golgotha. There they crucified him, and with him two others, one on either side, and Jesus between them" (John 19:16–18). And as the little girl listened and heard this for the first time, she buried her face in her mother's coat and wept, and cried out so that in the stillness of the church everyone heard her voice, "Why did they do it? Why did they do it?" It seemed to her the most terrible thing she had ever heard. Paul drove in upon his hearers what a shocking crime the crucifixion of Jesus was and we must try to feel something of its horror.

Conquest and triumph

But Paul did not stop with the crucifixion. In verses 30–37 he goes on to tell of the triumph of the Resurrection and of how it was all foretold by the prophets long ago. To the people in the early Church, the Resurrection was all important, because it meant so many great things. For one thing, it meant that the wickedness of men could do its worst to Jesus and yet in the end he triumphed. For another thing, it meant that he was not dead but alive. He was not a figure in a story; he was someone they could meet. The biggest mistake we can make about Jesus is to think of him as a figure in history who lived and died and was finished. He is someone who is with us every day.

When Paul in verses 33–36 tries to prove all this by quoting the Psalms and the prophets, it is difficult for us nowadays to grasp his argument. But by quoting the prophecies of ancient men, Paul insists that history is not haphazard. If there is such a thing as prophecy, if men could look forward to the coming of Jesus and the death of Jesus and the Resurrection of Jesus, it means that history is an orderly process. It is told that on a particularly stormy night, when a gale was blowing, a child once said, "I think God must have lost control of his winds to-night." The very fact that prophecy was possible at all was to Paul the guarantee that God never loses control of history and that his hand is always on the helm.

The offer of forgiveness

In verses 38 and 39 Paul goes on to tell just what this means. Because Jesus lived and suffered and died, there is forgiveness for men. We remember how the crowd rejected Jesus and chose Barabbas. John Oxenham has imagined how Barabbas felt about it. Barabbas was a revolutionary and very probably a murderer too, but something about Jesus fastened on his mind and he followed him to see the end. All the time he was thinking, "If it had not been for him, it would have been I who would have been crucified there." He felt that Jesus was bearing the punishment he should have borne. Paul always felt that because God is so perfect and we are so imperfect, we can never deserve anything but punishment from him; and he felt that in some wonderful way the punishment that we should have borne fell upon Jesus and put us right with God.

The threat

In verses 40 and 41 Paul finishes with a threat. It is as if he said, said, "If you miss this chance and refuse this offer, then you yourself are to blame for what may happen to you." When Bunyan was still not a Christian, he tells us, one day he was playing tip-cat on the village green and, clear as could be, he heard a voice saying at his elbow, "Wilt thou leave thy sins and go to heaven or wilt thou have thy sins and go to hell?" Paul and Bunyan knew that it was going to make all the difference in this world and in the world to come if they took Jesus as Master and Lord.

That is the outline of the first missionary sermon of which we have any record. It stresses God's plan in history; the witness of the greatest men of the time to Jesus; the terrible crime of the crucifixion; the triumph of the Resurrection; the forgiveness of God through Jesus Christ; and the choice that every man must make.

CHAPTER TWELVE

Expelled Out of their Coasts

Expelled from Antioch in Pisidia

It was as a sick man that Paul had first come to Pisidian Antioch. In his weakness he had come there to escape the malaria of the low-lying coastal districts. Pisidian Antioch was 3,600 feet up and the clean, clear air of the mountain plateau soon revived his strength. So after that first Sabbath in the synagogue Paul was able to throw himself into the work of preaching and teaching and debating with redoubled vigour. The sermon he had preached in the synagogue had been mightily effective and had made a tremendous impression on the minds of all who heard it.

We must remind ourselves of the passion for words which that age had. A really great orator had a following in those days as a great actor has in our day; and vast crowds would assemble anywhere to hear great speech and great debating. For a week the city was in a ferment discussing this new religion that Paul had brought. On the next Sabbath it seemed that the whole population of Antioch had tried to pack itself into the synagogue.

Now the real significance of the matter began to dawn on the Jews. They began to see that all this involved the claim that they were no longer the sole possessors of the grace and favour of God, but that the door to God's heart and to God's Kingdom was wide open to the Gentiles, whom they had regarded as liable only to his contempt, his anger and his hatred of God. They could not endure it in silence. They did everything to contradict, interrupt and silence Paul and Barnabas.

Paul and Barnabas put the matter beyond all conjecture. They told the Jews that they had had their chance; God's offer in Jesus Christ had been made to them; they had rejected it; and now it was to be taken to the Gentiles. This utterly infuriated them. Try to imagine how they felt. Centuries of regarding themselves as the chosen people had given them a certain mental arrogance. They looked on God as their exclusive possession; and on the Gentiles as less than the dust; and now they were being asked to believe that the despised Gentiles were as dear to God as they were.

They themselves could take no decisive action; but they could and did arrange that it should be taken. Many Gentiles had been in the former days converts to the Jewish faith, and especially a large number of women had accepted Jewish beliefs. That was because of the moral purity of Judaism. The heathen had relaxed the marriage bond until it counted for very little; Judaism taught purity and fidelity between the sexes. The Jews approached certain women who had been attenders at the synagogue. These women were wives of the magistrates of the city. They succeeded in persuading them to influence their husbands to expel Paul and Barnabas from Antioch and from the surrounding district. So the law took its course and by decree of the magistrates Paul and Barnabas were expelled.

Here we have a pattern of events which became familiar in the career of Paul. Over and over again it was the same. The Jews bitterly and angrily and even savagely resented the offer of God's grace to the Gentiles; and over and over again they engineered affairs so that Paul and his fellow-missionaries were persecuted and hindered.

On to Iconium

So Paul and Barnabas left Pisidian Antioch and went eighty miles on to Iconium, a proud and ancient city which claimed to be older than Damascus. One of its mythical kings in the days before history was called Nannacus; and there was a proverb, "since the days of Nannacus", which meant, "from the very beginning of time."

If they had ever any doubt before, they must now have been quite certain that wherever they went they were taking their lives in their hands. Yet it never even struck them to turn back. In the

Iliad, Homer tells of Achilles being told by the prophetess that if he goes out to a certain battle he will be killed. "Nevertheless," answers the Greek hero, "I am for going on." No matter what lay ahead, Paul and Barnabas were for going on.

In Iconium, Paul, as ever, began in the synagogue. The impact of this new message was even more startling than it had been in Antioch. The result of the preaching was that the whole city was divided into two hostile factions. Men took their religion with a certain violence in those days. There were fights such as might come nowadays between the supporters of two rival football teams. In the end Paul and Barnabas were in serious danger of being lynched and had to flee for their lives.

We must note one thing. The farther Paul and Barnabas penetrated into Asia Minor's inner fastnesses, the farther they got from civilisation. Life became even more dangerous. They had been expelled from Antioch by magisterial decree; they were driven from Iconium by a threat of mob lynching. Paul and Barnabas were not now risking what one might call a respectable imprisonment; they were risking being torn in pieces by excitable Phrygian mobs wrought up to a frenzy of passion by the subtle machinations of the Jews.

On to Lystra

The cities were now behind Paul and Barnabas. They were going out into a country so wild, so desert, so remote that there were places where water was actually sold for money. So they came to Lystra, a town famous because it was the end of the Roman Road. It is amazing to see how Paul would go anywhere to preach Christ. He would cheerfully enter the greatest cities in the world and he would equally cheerfully set out to the wild, remote places which were quite literally at the end of the civilised world.

In Lystra there was a certain difficulty. There the Greek language was not nearly so well understood. Lystra was far off the beaten track. It was much more difficult for Paul and Barnabas in this kind of place to establish contact between themselves and the people who were their audience. Nor was there any Jewish synagogue in Lystra. Here Paul and Barnabas had a new kind of problem to solve. They preached, but preaching by itself seems to have had little effect. But when they were preaching one day in the market square, Paul noticed a man who had been born a cripple. There was something about him which made it clear to Paul that he had a wistful yearning to be healed and a dawning consciousness of the power of this new gospel. Crisply and authoritatively Paul bade him, who had never stood, to stand; and, to his amazement, the man found himself able to rise and walk. If he was amazed, no less were the rest of the people.

Immediately their minds began to work. In that district of Lycaonia there was an old legend and an old belief. Long, long ago, when the world was young and the gods walked amongst men, two of the gods, Jupiter and Mercury, had come to Lycaonia, but in disguise. Through the country they had wandered seeking food and refuge and shelter and for long they had found none to give it to them. They had found every door shut in their faces. But at length they came to a cottage where a peasant called Philemon lived a simple life with his wife Baucis. These two welcomed the two strangers and gave them such simple hospitality as they were able to supply. The result was that Jupiter and Mercury revealed their true identity to Philemon and Baucis. The rest of the Lycaonians who had refused hospitality to the divine visitors were sorely punished; but Philemon and Baucis were greatly honoured. They were made the caretakers of a noble temple that was erected to Jupiter and when they were old and near to death they were turned into two great trees which stood before the shrine.

When the people of Lystra saw the wonder that Paul had worked for the lame man they at once leaped to the conclusion that history had repeated itself, and that the gods had come again. Because Barnabas was tall and handsome and grave and dignified they took him for Jupiter, the king of the gods. Because Paul was the man of words, they took him for Mercury, who was the god of speech and the messenger of the gods. And straightway the priest of Jupiter set on foot arrangements for all due sacrifices to be made to Barnabas and Paul.

For some little time Paul and Barnabas did not realise what was happening and then it became clear. Immediately they told the people that this must not be; that sacrifice to the heathen gods was the very thing they had come to tell them was at an end; that the old days of ignorance were past; that the God who had ever given them the sun and the rain and the seasons was now come to reveal himself to them; and that it was that true God whom they had come to preach.

There was immediate confusion. We can well understand a certain resentment in the hearts of the people of Lystra. They had been all set to welcome immortal gods and the celebrations were abruptly interrupted. They were both bewildered and annoyed. They felt like men who had been made to look foolish, and no one likes that.

Things might have been straightened out but a new factor entered in. It was late summer, the time of the harvest. It was always the custom of Antioch and Iconium to send people into the interior at that time to buy corn. Just at that most inopportune moment these merchants arrived. We may well imagine their feelings. Paul and Barnabas had been expelled from Antioch by magisterial decree; they had been chased from Iconium by the threat of lynching; and here were this pestilential pair still at it, undaunted and unsilenced and in a fair way to being recognised as gods.

These Jews acted quickly. They stirred up the already disgruntled people and in no time stones were flying. Paul was hit by a stone with full force and dropped senseless. Now the mob were shocked back to their senses. Lystra might be far away; but Lystra was under Roman law; Roman law had a long arm and took a grim view of breaches of the peace where stones flew and lives were lost. So the people of Lystra took the senseless Paul and dragged, as they thought, his dead body outside the city wall so that it might appear that he had met his death there and not inside the city.

But Paul was not dead; he was only stunned. Slowly he came back to his senses and no sooner were his wits about him again than "he rose up and came into the city." Here is courage of a matchless sort. Paul had just been stoned and dragged out of the city for dead; and the first thing he did was to walk straight back into that city to face again the men who had stoned him. There is little anyone can say about a cool courage like that. It is the highest form of courage. It was not reckless courage; it was courage which knew all the dangers and faced them.

Many and many a time John Wesley in later days was in peril of his life. He had only one rule when men threatened his life— "Always look a mob in the face." That was Paul's rule too. It was at Lystra that Paul made one of his most notable converts, a young man whom he called one day his son in the faith, a young man named Timothy (Acts 16:1). It may well be that it was this display of courage which thirled Timothy to Paul.

So, then, the perils mount up. Paul had been expelled from Antioch by the magistrates; he had left Iconium when there was every chance of his being lynched; and in Lystra he had faced the mob till he was stoned into unconsciousness.

Derbe

There was but one other town that Paul could visit. It was the town of Derbe. Derbe was on the very frontiers of the province of Galatia and there was no farther to go because the road stopped there. It seems that there Paul had peace and good success at the end of his troubled journey.

The way back

After his time in Derbe, Paul started on the way back, through Lystra, Iconium, and Antioch to Perga where this time he was strong enough to preach. At each place he stopped and encouraged those who had become Christian, gathering them into little communities and appointing elders in each of them to administer the affairs of the young congregations.

We may note two things about this.

(*a*) In each town there had arisen a Christian community. The Christian as soon as he was a Christian became a member of a fellowship, a congregation. The Christian life is not meant to be lived alone. It is always meant to be lived in a community.

It would be difficult to practise the Christian virtues alone. Love, charity, the forgiving spirit, honesty, honour—all these are things to be lived out amidst a community of fellow Christians. When Wesley first became a Christian he proposed to build a cabin on the Yorkshire moors and there spend all his days alone, withdrawn from the fellowship of men, in prayer and meditation. An older and wiser Christian said to him, "God knows nothing of solitary religion." We are to live out our Christianity amongst our fellow men and in the Christian community which is the Church.

(*b*) In each town elders were appointed. From the first the Church needed its leaders. A community cannot well exist without them. In those early Christian communities there emerged at once men who had gifts, men who were obviously in earnest, men who were prepared to give their time and their work to the service of the Church. The Church still needs men like that.

The return

When the work in Perga was done, Paul and Barnabas sought ship at the Pamphylian port of Attaleia. From there they sailed to Seleuceia at the mouth of the Orontes and then journeyed the fifteen miles up the river to Antioch. What a story they had to tell! Only it was not the story of what they had done but of "what God had done with them." They knew that they had been instruments in his hands. (Acts 14:27). So ended the first missionary journey which saw Paul begin a career of perils which was to last until he died.

CHAPTER THIRTEEN

Come Over and Help Us

The cities of Paul

So far we have been trying to trace Paul's life from month to month and from year to year. We cannot continue to do that because such an investigation would take up more space and time than we have at our disposal. So now we are going to adopt a new method and look at Paul against the background of certain of the great cities where he lived and worked.

A momentous decision

When Paul came back from his first missionary journey he gave a report of all that he and Barnabas had done; and the Church ratified his actions. Once and for all it was decided that the gospel was for every man, and that Jew and Gentile alike must be admitted without let or hindrance into the fellowship of the Christian Church (Acts 15). But the wanderlust was in Paul's blood. He must be going on and ever on. So he set out again, and at first he went to revisit and to strengthen and to encourage the churches which he knew and loved so well.

There came a time when Paul did not clearly know what to do or where to go. He had gone through Syria and Cilicia and Phrygia and Galatia and he was looking for new lands to conquer for Christ. Very simply but very dramatically in Acts 16:6–8 Luke tells the story of what happened next. As we read these verses we have a sense of some great power driving Paul relentlessly on. He might have gone into the teeming province of Asia but something stopped him; he might have turned aside to the cities of Bithynia but something barred his way; and so, as if driven to it, he came to Alexandrian Troas and the shores of the Aegean Sea. Even there he was in doubt. He had gone to bed turning the problem over in his mind and in the night there came to him a vision and he saw a man from Macedonia who entreated him, "Come over to Macedonia and help us."

The Gospel comes to Europe

Now the period of indecision was over, the way lay straight before him and Paul took ship for Europe. It was a great step.

So far Christianity had been an Eastern religion. Born in Palestine, it had spread throughout Asia Minor but now the first step was taken to the invasion of the West. *We* ourselves owe our Christianity to the decision Paul took that day to set sail for Macedonia.

Philippi

He landed at Neapolis and twelve miles inland there lay Philippi, an ancient and a famous city. Long centuries ago it had been called Crenides which means "The Springs." But Philip of Macedon, the father of Alexander the Great, had rebuilt and fortified it to be a defence for Macedonia against the marauding Thracians. In those days it had famous gold mines which were a great source of riches.

Three more centuries passed on and when Julius Caesar was murdered the fate of the Roman Empire and of the world was in the balance. Was the world to be ruled by Augustus, Caesar's adopted heir, or was it to be ruled by Brutus and Cassius, who had assassinated Caesar? It was at Philippi that the decisive battle was fought and in that battle Augustus was victorious. It was little wonder that he regarded Philippi with affection and made it a Roman colony.

Dotted all over the world there were Roman colonies. These colonies were little models of Rome. The Roman citizens who settled in them wore Roman dress; they spoke the Latin tongue; they had their own Roman magistrates. Wherever these places were, they were Roman and proud of it. Such was Philippi. As Paul walked its streets he would see everywhere the initials S.P.Q.R. which stood for "The Senate and the People of Rome."

He would see the statue of Augustus. Everything would make him think of Rome. Somehow in Philippi the conquest of Rome for Christ must have become a reality with him.

The all-embracing Gospel

The story of Paul's work in Philippi is in Acts 16:12–40 and nowhere is the universal appeal of the gospel of Christ more clearly seen. In that chapter we read specially of three people who were brought to Christ, and they come from every point of the social scale.

The seller of purple

First there was the lady whom the Revised Standard Version calls Lydia (Acts 16:12–14). More likely we do not know her name. Lydia is not a proper name but means "The Lydian," or "The Lady from Lydia." She came from Thyatira, a city in the province of Lydia, which was famous the world over for its purple dye. The Lydian lady was a seller of purple and she must have been exceedingly rich. The Romans specially valued purple dye which came from a little shellfish and had to be collected a drop at a time. Kings, magistrates and commanders in the field wore purple robes. Magistrates, senators and knights wore their togas with a purple border. So precious was this purple dye that a pound of wool dyed with it cost as much as £50. The Lydian lady was the equivalent of a financial magnate or a captain of commerce; and yet, wealthy as she was, she committed herself to Jesus Christ.

The demented girl

As Paul went through the streets of Philippi he had a strange experience with a poor mad girl. The ancient peoples had a very special respect for those who were mad. They said that the gods had taken their wits away to give them heavenly wisdom. This girl was what was called a Pytho and had the natural gift of ventriloquism. Her masters used her for fortune telling, and made money out of her misfortune. Somehow or other something about Paul fascinated this girl and she kept following him about, crying out that he was the servant of the most high God and had come to show people the way to salvation. At last Paul turned and spoke to her with that commanding personality of his and with the power that Jesus gave to him. Her poor troubled mind became sane again (Acts 16:16–18), and Paul had won another for Christ.

The Philippian gaoler

You would have thought that anyone would be glad that such a deed had been done and that a poor demented girl had got her wits back. But her masters were enraged because they could no longer make money out of her. So they took their revenge in a very subtle way.

Roman colonies prided themselves that, whatever might happen elsewhere, there was never a disturbance or a breach of the peace in them. So these masters dragged Paul and his friends before the Roman magistrates and charged them with being disturbers of the peace. The magistrates in colonies were apt to be very self-important and very proud of their office. Without taking any evidence, they beat Paul and his friends and flung them into prison. The beating was done by men called lictors; the lictors carried rods and it was with these rods that Paul and the others were beaten.

They were not only put into prison but into the inner prison. Very likely it was a dark dungeon below the level of the ground. They were not only put there but were put in the stocks. Probably the stocks were such that not only their feet but their hands and heads also were fixed so that they could not move. But that was not enough to daunt Paul and Silas, and even at midnight they were singing hymns of praise. The magistrates could put them in prison but they could not separate them from the presence of Jesus, their Lord.

Philippi was a place where there were a great many earthquakes which made the ground tremble and the houses shake. There came an earthquake that night the shock of which jerked open the stocks and lifted the bar of the door right out of its supports, and all that Silas and Paul had to do was to walk out. In came the gaoler, terrified. According to Roman law, if a prisoner escaped the gaoler himself must suffer the punishment the prisoner would have suffered. No wonder he was afraid. But Paul and Silas made no effort to escape. The bewildered gaoler by this time was sure that his captives were more than ordinary men and he came to them, asking, "What must I do to be saved?" So Paul and Silas told him all about Jesus, and that night the gaoler became a Christian and all his household with him.

Here we have the third person whom Paul brought to Christ. First there was the wealthy Lydian lady; then there was the homeless, penniless slave-girl: now there was the gaoler, a respectable Roman civil servant, a good middle-class citizen. From every point of the social scale people were taking Jesus as their Master and their Lord (Acts 16:19–33).

Paul stands on his rights

Morning came and the magistrates, perhaps scared by the earthquake, perhaps realising now that they had been a little hasty, sent a message to let Paul and Silas go. Paul sent back a message that must have given these petty magistrates the shock of their lives. "You never gave us a trial," he said. "You actually beat us with rods; *and we are Roman citizens.*" To beat a Roman citizen was a terrible crime. If Paul had liked to follow this matter up, he could have had these magistrates deposed and perhaps even executed, and well they knew it. "If you want us to leave prison," said Paul, "come and fetch us out and apologise in public for the public insult you have done to us." Paul took this line, not to glorify himself nor to get his own back. He took it because he knew he had to go away and the magistrates might have made life very unpleasant for the Christians he left behind, and he wanted to let them know that the Christians had influential friends behind them. So the magistrates came humbly and apologised and brought Paul and Silas out of prison. After Paul visited the house of the Lydian lady and met the Christians there he went on his way (Acts 16:35–40).

The universal Gospel

In Philippi the Lydian lady, the slave girl and the gaoler had all entered the Christian Church. Here was proof that there was room in the Church for everyone. There was nowhere else in the ancient world where people of all classes and conditions could come together. The Jews shut out the Gentiles. The Greeks described all other nations as barbarians. Aristotle had said that there were two kinds of people—those who were wise and cultured and intellectual and those who were fit for nothing but to be slaves, hewers of wood and drawers of water. And he said that it was wrong to try to educate the second class; they must be kept as slaves. The ancient world was a world of barriers. Only in the Christian Church were these barriers taken away.

We must never look with contempt on anyone; we must remember that the Christian Church is for everyone because God wants every man of every class, of every country and of every colour to know him and to love him.

G

CHAPTER FOURTEEN

The Marriage of the East and the West

The shadow of Alexander

Let us go back to Acts 16:6–8 again. A certain relentless pressure had driven Paul on the shores of the Aegean Sea and had brought him to Troas. There had come to him that vision which sent him over the sea to Macedonia. As events began to move, there must have been in Paul's mind all the time the thought of one man, and that perhaps the greatest the world has ever seen —Alexander the Great.

It would have been hard to forget him. The full name of Troas was Alexandrian Troas and it was called after Alexander. Philippi was called after Philip the father of Alexander. Thessalonica was called after the wife of Cassander, the half-sister of Alexander. Macedonia itself had been the native place of Alexander and the cradle from which his empire grew.

Alexander was the first and the greatest of the universalists. He had said himself that it was his aim "to marry the east to the west." He had actually taken ten thousand of his soldiers and married them to Persian girls. Often he had taken boys from the conquered nations and had them educated in Greek ways and Greek ideas. Aristotle had been the tutor of Alexander and he had declared that it was a plain duty to treat Greeks as free men and Orientals as slaves; but Alexander had replied that "he had been sent by God to unite, pacify and reconcile the whole world." Alexander had been the first man to conceive of a world without barriers. He had thought in terms of one world. And Paul must have been thinking of the man who had dreamed of a world empire for he was dreaming of a world for Christ.

The strategist's eye

Paul always had the eye of a general. He looked at a country and saw the bridgeheads he must win. He saw the strategic cities which would give him a whole territory and hinterland. Nowhere is that more evident than in his campaign for Christ in Macedonia. In those days when roads were few and bad, much of the trade and commerce passed down the river valleys; and the towns which commanded the rivers were the towns which commanded the whole territory. In Macedonia there were three rivers, the Strymon, the Axius and the Haliacmon. These three river valleys were commanded by three towns, Philippi, Thessalonica and Beroea. It was in these three towns that Paul flung down his challenge for Christ. When the Romans had conquered Macedonia they had divided it into three parts, First, Second and Third Macedonia. These three towns were the capitals of these three districts. If the word could be planted in them, it would inevitably expand through the whole district. Paul approached his Macedonian campaign with the eye of the master tactician.

On to Thessalonica

So after Paul had left Philippi he set out again for Thessalonica. Acts 17:1 is one of the verses which show us how little we really know of the work of Paul. That verse reads very simply, "Now when they passed through Amphipolis and Apollonia, they came to Thessalonica." Put like that, it sounds like a pleasant day's walk. But in point of fact Philippi to Amphipolis was 33 Roman miles; Amphipolis to Apollonia was 30 Roman miles; Apollonia to Thessalonica was 37 Roman miles. A journey of almost 100 miles is dismissed in a sentence. It was in fact a mere nothing for a man like Paul.

Thessalonica

So Paul came to Thessalonica and his arrival there was one of the hinges of history. Thessalonica had a long history. Six hundred years before this it had been a city. In those old days its name was Thermae, which means "The Hot Springs." But in 315 B.C. Cassander had rebuilt it and given it the name Thessalonica.

Thessalonica stood on the Thermaic gulf and was a famous harbour. When Xerxes invaded Greece he used Thessalonica as his naval base and even in Roman days it was famous for its dock-yards. In later days Thessalonica very nearly became the capital of the world because it was a narrow choice between it and Con-stantinople. It had a population of 200,000 people and even to this day it is a town of 70,000 inhabitants.

But it was none of these things which made Paul's arrival so epoch-making. The salient fact is this. Thessalonica stood astride the Egnatian Road. Now that Egnatian Road was one of the great Roman roads. It ran from Dyrrachium on the Adriatic to Constantinople and on to Asia Minor in the East. The whole east to west and west to east traffic of the world passed through Thessalonica. It was as Cicero said, "In the lap of the Roman Empire."

The significance is tremendous. Thessalonica was the bridge between the east and the west. Along that Egnatian Road, of which her very main street was part, Christianity could move east until it reached Constantinople and west until it reached Rome. The preaching of Christianity in Thessalonica was in a very real sense the beginning of the preaching of Christianity to the whole world. If Thessalonica was won for Christ, Christianity was planted at the very heart of the Roman Empire.

Events in Thessalonica

Now let us see what happened in Thessalonica. Paul began his campaign in the synagogue. There was a time when half the population of Thessalonica was Jewish and the synagogue must still have numbered thousands amongst its members. By begin-ning in the synagogue Paul had a double audience. First, he had the Jews themselves and to the end of the day Paul offered the gospel first to his own countrymen. But second, around every synagogue there had gathered a great crowd of Gentiles. They were dissatisfied at heart with the many gods of paganism and with the loose morality of the pagan life. In the one God of the Jews and in the strict Jewish code they found something that lifted life to new levels. So to this double audience Paul preached.

A few of the Jews believed, but with the Gentiles who were gathered round the synagogue Paul's success was startling. A great multitude of them were won for Christ. Immediately the Jews were infuriated. They had always regarded these Gentiles as their own special property and they had no intention of sitting and doing nothing about it while they were led away, as they thought by Paul.

Trouble at Thessalonica

The Jews took their revenge in a peculiarly underhand way. They collected "some wicked fellows of the rabble." The Greek word which describes these people literally means "men who stood about the market-place." "Corner boys" would be the English equivalent. With these gangsters they stirred up a riot. They assaulted the house of Jason where Paul had been staying; and they dragged Jason before the magistrates with certain of the Christians.

Thessalonica was a free city; it had never had the indignity of a Roman garrison quartered within its walls. So this was serious. Rome would stand many things, but riots she would not tolerate. She could not afford to with an empire her size. There must be no trouble spots where rebellion might begin.

To make it worse, these cunning and malicious Jews preferred a charge against the Christians of which the magistrates had to take account. They accused them of being revolutionaries and said they were attempting to set up another emperor, one Jesus by name. Jason and his friends were for the moment severely reprimanded and compelled to give security for their conduct; but for Paul the situation had become impossible and he had to be smuggled away by night to Beroea. Great things had happened in Thessalonica but they ended with Paul in peril of his life (Acts 17:1–10).

The power of the gospel

There are two things to be noted here. The first is the power of the gospel. The cry of the Thessalonian Jews was, "These men who have turned the world upside down have come here also."

That was meant as a slander but in fact it was the truth. It has been charged against Christianity that it is "the opiate of the people", that it is something to send people to sleep and make them accept things against which they should rise in wrath. The very opposite is true. Real Christianity is a disturbing thing.

It disturbs our own lives because it fills us with the feeling that the life we are living will not do. It disturbs social life because it insists that social evils and abuses must go. To take but one example, it was Christianity which put an end to slavery. T. R. Glover used to quote with great delight the story of the little girl who had not got things quite right and who insisted that the New Testament "ended in Revolutions"—and she was quite right. During the 1914–18 war the Quakers would not fight because their creed would not allow them; but they did noble service in the hospitals and among the wounded. They were not allowed to preach their creed to soldiers and they asked if they might be allowed to read the New Testament to them. The authorities agreed but reminded them that "there were occasions on which the New Testament was a highly dangerous book." Real Christianity is no opiate. It ought to be, as it was in Thessalonica, the most explosive force in the world.

The infection of Christianity

The second thing we have to note is even more important. Read Acts 17:2. The total time Paul spent in Thessalonica *cannot have been more than three weeks at the most*. This was of the most incalculable importance for the spread of Christianity. If Paul had to settle down in every city and spend months or even years before he could make any real impression, his task was near to being hopeless; but if in three weeks he could make Christianity run like wildfire through a community, then there was hope that the whole of the Empire might be won for Christ. Paul's heart must have leaped for joy when he found that in three weeks time he could light a fire that nothing could put out.

How was it done? It was done because Christianity spread like an infection from man to man. It was not done by preaching. It was done by the sheer power of a Christian life. It will always be true that Christianity can be caught more easily than it can be taught. There is no advertisement for it like the advertisement of a Christian life. There is no argument for it like the argument of a Christian person. We must show what Christianity is not by our words but by our lives.

H. L. Gee tells how he spent some time during World War I on a farm. The farmer and his wife, John and Mary, were real Christians with the grace of God in them. There was a landgirl on the farm, a modern young lady, who, when she arrived, had not the slightest use for Christianity. But bit by bit, by watching John and Mary, she began to see that there must be something in this business of being a Christian. When H. L. Gee was leaving, she said something like this to him, "I know now that there is something in Christianity. I try to read the Bible, but I find it very difficult. I try to pray, but I don't know the right words. But I'm not worrying because I know I'll find God by following Mary."

That is the way people find God. And if we would help God's kingdom, we must seek to spread our Christianity like an infection to the people whom we meet.

CHAPTER FIFTEEN

The Glory that was Greece

To Athens

When Paul left Thessalonica he went on to Beroea, but there also the plots and stratagems of the Jews compelled him to leave in haste and secrecy, and this time, all alone, he went to Athens. There had been a time when Athens had been the greatest city in the world, but the days of her greatness were gone. As one of her own writers said, "Nowadays she is like an old lady, sitting in carpet slippers, sipping barley water, by the fireside." Once Greece had been the most populous of countries but now that land which had been able to put whole armies into the field could scarcely have raised an expedition of three thousand men. Once Athens had been mistress of the seas, but a century before, when she had wished to send help to an admiral, she had been able to send only three ships. As a great scholar wrote of her, "She had played her part in the world's story—a part at once too glorious and too exhausting to be played a second time. And now her cultivated fields were lonely sheepwalks; her flourishing cities had dwindled to villages."

Athens and culture

But even if Greece was now negligible as a world power and her great days lay behind her, it still remained true that Athens was the greatest university city in the world and the home of learning and of philosophy. It was to Athens that people from all over the world came to finish their education.

The story of the rise of the University of Athens is one of the strangest in the world. Away back in 336 B.C. Greece had instituted compulsory military service. Boys of eighteen years of age had to do two years of compulsory military service where they were trained in the art of warfare and of gymnastics. But by the middle of the third century things changed. The compulsion ceased. Athens no longer needed soldiers and the courses in warfare and gymnastics were changed into courses in rhetoric and philosophy, and the young men, who a century before had been trained to be soldiers, were now trained to be scholars instead. The swords had been changed to ploughshares, the spears into pruning hooks and the manual of military tactics into the handbook of philosophy.

The spirit of Greece

The great characteristic of the Greek was that he had always been a seeker after knowledge. Above all, the Greeks were men of adventurous mind. As Luke himself wrote of them, they spent their time ever seeking to tell or to hear some new thing (Acts 17:21). They were born with the wanderlust. "I travelled," wrote Herodotus, one of their two great historians, "for no other reason than to learn and to inquire." Aristotle called curiosity the mother of philosophy. Celsus, a Greek, wrote an attack on Christianity. He said that it was possible that the barbarians might have some gift for discovering new truth, but, he said, "it takes a Greek to understand." The Greeks were born with curiosity in their souls. They loved discussion. It was a small matter whether or not the discussion reached any conclusion. What they wanted was "the stimulus of a mental hike," and the sheer exercise of the reason, the sheer sharpening of mind against mind was dear to the Greek heart. Athens was a city where men did nothing but talk. "You Greeks," said an Egyptian, "are like children; you are always young in your souls." Athens was a city of men who might have lost all claims to political greatness but who had never lost the adventurous mind. Into such a city of mental aristocrats went Paul, the little Jewish tentmaker.

Athens and the gods

But if Athens was a city of philosophers, still more was it a city of gods. It was, as Paul felt, a city filled with idols (Acts 17:16).

It was so full of statues of gods that one writer said there were more statues in Athens than in all the rest of Greece put together, while another declared that in Athens it was easier to meet a statue than it was to meet a man. And even when the whole regiment of gods had been exhausted they erected altars to the unknown gods.

There was a time six hundred years before this when a pestilence had fallen on Athens, and even when sacrifice had been made to every known god, the pestilence still raged. A Cretan poet, Epimenides, came forward with a plan. He ordered a flock of black and white sheep to be collected; they were driven to the hill known as the Areiopagus, and then were let loose throughout the city. Wherever each lay down it was sacrificed to the nearest god; and if a sheep lay down near to the shrine of no known god, it was sacrified to "The Unknown Gods." So, the story went, Athens was freed from her pestilence.

There is a certain pathos in the thought that deep in the Greek mind was this almost unexpressed feeling that beyond the gods they knew there must be others whose power was greater than them all and whose hands were on the helm of things. Into this city of strange gods came Paul, schooled in the faith of the one true God and member of a nation whose law it was that no graven image must be made.

Paul and the philosophers

It would seem that when Paul came to Athens he did not mean to preach very much. He was waiting there only until Timothy could catch up on him with news from Thessalonica; but Paul could never keep silence if there were folk to whom he could speak of Jesus Christ.

He began, as he always did, by discussing in the synagogue; but soon he had a far wider audience than that. The centre of Athens was the Agora, the great city square. It was at once the commercial, the social and the intellectual centre of the city. There were the merchants driving their bargains; the idlers talking the time away; the philosophers talking of deep things or splitting hairs.

Let us think of the scenes with which Paul was surrounded. On the south was the Pnyx. It was a gently sloping hill hollowed out into a flat place. It was there that the great meetings of the Athenian people had been held and where decisions that had moved the world had been taken. History was looking down on Paul. On the north there was the Areiopagus, the hill of Mars, crowned with the statue of Mars. It was there that the most ancient court of the Athenians met, the court which had the over-sight of public morals and public religion, the court which had condemned Socrates to death. The judges of Greece looked down on Paul. On the east was the Acropolis, one solid mass of temples and of statues. There in the niches of the hill were the shrines of Bacchus and of Aesculapius, of Venus and of Ceres and above all the great gleaming, glittering statue of Minerva, made with the bronze of the shields and the weapons captured at Marathon, whose glint could be seen far out at sea as ships approached the anchorage of Athens. There was scarcely a Greek god who did not look down on Paul. Now, if ever, Paul needed that courage of his to make him not ashamed of the gospel of Christ.

Any wandering philosopher could gather a crowd in the Agora and before long Paul was the centre of an interested group. Amongst them were Stoics and Epicureans (Acts 17:18). These were the two great schools of philosophy in the time of Paul. Let us see what they believed so that we can see what Paul was up against.

The Stoic faith

The Stoics believed that God was fiery spirit and that every-thing in all the world was quite literally God. They believed that at its highest tension that fiery spirit was God. Then they had the curious belief that when that fiery spirit became a little less tense it became air; when it became still more dull it became water; when it became altogether dull and heavy it became matter. They believed that what gave a man power to live and to think was that a particle of that fiery spirit had come to live in him and that when he died it went back to God and was absorbed in him. So the Stoics lived in a world which was full of God and literally was God.

They believed that in the world there was a plan and that life consisted in putting yourself in line with that plan. Happiness was obtainable only when a man submitted his whole will to that plan. They believed that everything happened for the best and that therefore it must be accepted; and so they laid down the rule that if we cannot get what we want we must train ourselves to want what we can get.

They further believed that God was *apathetic*. When we use that word we mean *indifferent*; but they meant *incapable of any feeling whatever*. They argued that if a person has feelings it means that someone else can make him glad or sad, happy or unhappy. That means the other person can influence him; and if he can influence him, he is for the moment the greater. But, they said, no one can be greater than God, therefore no one can influence him, therefore God must be incapable of any feeling whatsoever.

They urged men to become the same, to try to reach a stage when they could say of anything, "I don't care." One of their teachers said, "Begin with a cup or a dress; if you break it or tear it, say, 'I don't care.' Go on to a pet dog or animal; if it is hurt or killed, say, 'I don't care.' Go on to your own serious illness and if you break your leg or arm, say, 'I don't care.' And finally you will come to a state when you can see your child suffer or your wife die, and say, 'I don't care.' " The Stoic urged men to banish every particle of feeling from their hearts. They tried to make of the human heart a desert and to call it peace.

Think how these men would feel when Paul spoke of a God who was *love*. To them it was the very opposite of all they believed.

The Epicureans

The Epicureans declared that the sole end of life was pleasure. By that they did not mean the pleasures of the body and the cheaper and more harmful pleasures. They took the long view and included not only the pleasure of the moment but also the effect it would have afterwards. In that sense virtue brought the greatest pleasure because in the long run it brought the greatest happiness. But the Epicureans believed that the greatest enemy of happiness was fear and especially fear of death. So they said that everything came into being in the following way. In the beginning there were nothing but atoms. These atoms were falling like rain through space. They might have gone on falling forever but they were endowed with the power to swerve. When they did swerve they knocked into each other and stuck to each other and out of these chance conglomerations of atoms, men and women and everything else were formed. They went on to say that when we die we simply disintegrate again into atoms and after death there is nothing at all. The Epicureans said there might be gods but they lived in the spaces between the worlds and were not in the least interested in men.

Think how these men must have felt when Paul spoke of God caring for men and of life after death.

Paul on trial

In point of fact when Paul did speak to these philosophers they misunderstood him. The Revised Standard Version has it that they thought he was preaching Jesus and the *resurrection*. The Greek for resurrection is *Anastasis*, and in Greek that could possibly be a female name. They thought that Paul was preaching about two new gods, Jesus and Anastasis. Now the court called the Areiopagus which met on the hill of the same name had the grave duty of giving judgment at murder trials and in cases which had anything to do with public morality and public religion. To that court Paul was hailed to answer for introducing new gods into the life of Athens (Acts 17:18).

Paul's speech before the Areiopagus

Paul's speech before the Areiopagus is given to us in Acts 17:22–31. He said he had come to tell them about that very unknown God to whom they erected their altars. He swept round on the many temples and statues and declared that the real God did not dwell in temples made with hands and needed no images for his worship. He told them that in previous days God had forgiven all this because men did not know any better; but that Jesus had now come who would one day judge the world and who gave us the assurance that there was a life after death.

The reaction of the Greeks

The Greeks met his speech in three different ways (Acts 17: 32–34).

(*a*) Some of them laughed at the whole business. It is still possible to laugh at Christianity. To put it in another way, it is still possible not to take it seriously enough. But Christianity is the most important thing in the world. Only when we give God the first place do all other things take their proper place.

(*b*) Some of them said, "We will hear you again about this." They were the people who put things off. To-morrow is the most dangerous word in the English language. There is a kind of parable about three apprentice devils who were coming to this earth to train. They were telling Satan what they proposed to do. One said, "I will tell men there is no God." Satan said, "That will not do because in their heart of hearts they know there is a God." The second said, "I will tell men there is no hell." Satan said, "That will not do because men have their regrets and their remorse and they have already tasted their own punishment." The third said, "I will tell men that *there is no hurry*." "Go," said Satan, "and you will ruin men by the million." It may well be that to-morrow will never come and there are some things so important that they should never be put off.

(*c*) Some few of them believed. They believed that what Paul said was true; and they made up their minds to mould their lives to fit his message.

Ourselves

When we hear of Jesus and his truth we may refuse to take them seriously; or we may put off coming to a decision to some other time; or we may accept him as our Master and our Lord. And we know which way is right.

CHAPTER SIXTEEN

The City of the Two Seas

Paul comes to Corinth

When Paul left Athens he came to Corinth. He could have gone overland but it was a stiff journey of forty difficult miles via the towns of Eleusis and Megara and it is more likely that he saved his tired body such an effort by taking ship and making the five-hour journey across the Saronic Gulf to the port of Cenchrea. We have already pointed out that Paul had a general's eye for the strategic centre and the vital bridgehead. A great scholar has said that it is a very illuminating fact that to this day many of the towns which Paul visited and in which he preached are still great ports and great road-centres.

Corinth

Of all strategic centres Corinth was the most commanding. A glance at the map will show how important a centre it was. Greece is almost cut in two by the sea. On one side there is the Saronic Gulf with its port of Cenchrea and on the other there is the Corinthian Gulf with its port of Lechaeum. Between the two lies a narrow isthmus of land only a few miles across and on that isthmus stands Corinth. Men called it "The City of two Seas." They spoke of it as "The Bridge of Greece," for every single item of traffic and of commerce that did not travel by sea had to pass through Corinth on its journey from north to south. One of the Greeks called it "The Lounge of Greece," where all men met.

Not only did north and south traffic pass through it; east and west traffic had to take the same route. The extreme southern point of Greece is called Cape Malea and, in ancient days, to sail round Cape Malea was the equivalent of sailing round Cape Horn in the days of sail. It was a journey so dangerous that there were two famous Greek proverbs, "Let him who sails round Malea forget his home," and, "Let him who thinks of sailing round Malea make his will." So what happened was this. Ships on their way from east to west or west to east sailed up one of the gulfs between which the isthmus stood. The isthmus was called the Diolkos, which means the place of dragging across. If the ship was small enough, it was set on rollers and dragged to the gulf on the other side. If it was too large for that, its cargo was disembarked and carried across and then re-embarked on a ship on the other side. So to escape the dreaded Cape Malea all east to west traffic passed through Corinth until men called it "The Market Place of Greece." Into its port, as has been written, came "Arabian balsam, Egyptian papyrus, Phoenician dates, Libyan ivory, Babylonian carpets, Cilician goats-hair, Lycaonian wool, Phrygian slaves." The ships from all the world found their way into the quays of Corinth, where the triremes, the famous ships of Greece, had first been built.

The Isthmian games

Not only was Corinth famous for its geographical position it had other claims to fame. Its history falls into two parts. In the old Greek days it had been famous but in 146 B.C. disaster had befallen it. At that time the Romans had conquered Greece, and doubtless because it was so important a strategic centre, had destroyed it stone by stone. A Greek historian tells how he saw the rough Roman soldiers using priceless pictures as draught boards and to Rome were brought vast amounts of carvings and statues, vases and objects of art which opened a new world of beauty to that less cultured city.

But in 44 B.C. it had risen again from the ruins. Julius Caesar had seen that the site of Corinth was far too important to lie desolate and a new and even more gorgeously luxurious town had risen on the ruins of the old.

One of its most famous functions was the Isthmian games,

second in fame only to the supreme Olympic games. It seems likely that Paul had attended these Isthmian games. From all over Greece people came to them and Paul would never have lost the opportunity of preaching the gospel to a crowd like that.

We may be sure that there was something of the sportsman in Paul. We can tell what kind of a man a man is by the kind of metaphors he uses to make his meaning plain, and scholars point out how there is hardly a contest in the games which Paul does not use as a metaphor to light up the Christian life. He knew about the contests of the boxers (1 Corinthians 9:26). He knew how the beasts fought in the arena; perhaps he had fought with them himself (1 Corinthians 15:32). It is interesting to note that Athens would never allow the gladiatorial games within her walls so long as there was a statue to the god of Pity in her temples.

But it is to the foot-race that so many of Paul's pictures owe their vividness. There is the herald who summons the runners to the starting-point (1 Corinthians 9:27); the course along which the athletes press on to their goal (Philippians 3:14); the judge awarding the prize at the end of the race (2 Timothy 4:8); the prize of the laurel crown for the victorious runner (1 Corinthians 9:24); the joy and exultation of the victor (Philippians 4:1); the rigorous discipline of training which the athlete must go through (1 Timothy, 4:7, 8); and the strict regulations which must be meticulously observed (2 Timothy 2:5).

It is clear that there was in Paul's character a real man's delight in the athlete's performance and power. So we may think of Paul as not only a spectator but a preacher at those games where half of Greece assembled.

The wicked city

There was still more to Corinth. It was one of the wickedest cities in the world. There was actually a Greek word "to play the Corinthian" which meant to live in drunken and immoral debauchery. The word in fact came into the English language and a "Corinthian" in regency times was one of those roystering young men who lived the wild life to the full. We are told that if

H

ever Corinthians were shown on the stage in ancient times, it was customary to make them appear as drunk.

Above all, on the Acropolis there was the Temple of Aphrodite. The Acropolis was a rock, two thousand feet high, dominating the isthmus. It was a great fortress, for he who possessed it commanded the isthmus and had all the trade routes at his mercy. But it was also the shrine of the Greek goddess of love. Her temple had a thousand priestesses who were sacred prostitutes and for the profit of the goddess they descended to the streets each evening and plied their immoral trade. It had indeed become a Greek proverb, "Not every man can afford a journey to Corinth." It was not only the open vices which flourished in Corinth, but the foreign sailors and traders coming from the ends of the earth brought in with them strange and recondite vices until Corinth became at one and the same time a synonym for luxury and for filth.

Paul in Corinth

In Corinth Paul spent longer witnessing for Christ than in any other city except Ephesus. When he arrived there he found lodging with a Jew and his wife, Aquila and Priscilla. They, too, were tentmakers, and Paul worked with them, for he was too proud to accept charity from and church or any man and insisted always on paying his own way. At first he was alone; and as usual he began by preaching in the synagogue. When Timothy and Silas arrived from Macedonia, Paul decided that the Jews had had their chance and that now he must go out to the Gentiles and tell them of the love of God (Acts 18:1–6). With characteristic audacity he took up his lodgings with a man called Justus who lived next door to the synagogue! There was a part of Paul's nature which would find a grim humour in living next door to the very people who were his sworn enemies.

Now Corinth was the capital of the province of Achaia and the seat of the Roman governor. To it came a new governor called Gallio, a man famed for the sweetness and the justice of his nature. His brother Seneca wrote of him, "Even those who love my brother Gallio to the utmost of their power do not love him enough." The Jews determined that they would try to take advantage of Gallio's newness to his job, and they brought Paul to his judgement seat. They accused him of teaching men to worship God contrary to the law. But Gallio was neither to be rushed or intimidated. He said, "If these men had been criminals or wrong-doers or immoral people, I would deal with this. But they are not. This is only a private quarrel of your own. Settle it yourselves." And he bade them be gone. Then with a kind of rough justice the Greek crowd took Sosthenes the ruler of the synagogue, with his fellow Jews, and beat them up. The Romans were far too just and far too impartial to allow themselves to be used as tools for the schemes of the Jews. So Paul lived and worked and taught in Corinth for almost two years.

Christianity in impossible circumstances

Of all the places in the world there cannot have seemed a less likely field for Christianity than Corinth; and yet there, in the most impossible circumstances, Paul witnessed for Christ. By so doing he demonstrated that it is possible for a man who is in earnest to be a Christian under any circumstances.

Hugh Redwood tells of a boy from a slum home in London who was taken away by Christian people to a summer camp. When the first meal was set before him, it was the finest he had ever seen in his life and he was about to fall upon it greedily. He was stopped and told that grace must first be said. It seemed to him a shocking waste of time; but bit by bit, as the days went on, he began to understand what grace before meat meant. He returned home. At the first meal in his own house he stood up and sang his grace. His father promptly knocked him down. "We want none of that nonsense here," he said, only he did not say it as politely as that. At the next meal the lad stood and began to sing his grace again. This time his brother knocked him down even more emphatically. At the next meal he stood again to sing his grace. His brother was just about to knock him down again when his father said, "Stop it. He's got more courage than you anyway. Let him alone."

Sometimes we think it is hard to be a Christian. It was harder still for that lad. It was harder even than that in Corinth; but if we are in earnest it is possible to be a Christian in any circumstances.

Such were some of you

Further, Paul proved by his stay in Corinth that Christianity can change even the worst kind of people. There is a wonderful passage in Paul's first letter to his friends at Corinth. "Do you not know that the unrighteous will not inherit the kingdom of God? Do not be deceived; neither the immoral, nor idolaters, nor adulterers, nor homosexuals, nor thieves, nor the greedy, nor drunkards, nor revilers, nor robbers will inherit the kingdom of God. *And such were some of you*" (1 Corinthians 6:9–11). In Corinth Paul demonstrated beyond all argument that Christ has the power to make bad men good. We may have habits which are difficult to overcome. We may have natures which are hard to control. But if we take Jesus as Master and Lord, he can do for us what we could never do for ourselves and he can make us what we could never make ourselves.

CHAPTER SEVENTEEN

The Vanity Fair of Asia Minor

Ephesus

For the time being Paul now left Europe and returned to Asia Minor; and the next of the great cities which he besieged for Christ was Ephesus. Ephesus stood in that part of Asia Minor which had been described by one of the great Greek historians as the best site in the world and had been called "The most magnificent of the magnificent cities of Asia".

The market of the world

In those days, as we saw when we were thinking of Macedonia, trade and commerce tended to travel down the river valleys; and Ephesus, at the mouth of the Cayster, commanded the trade of one of the richest hinterlands in all Asia. More than that, it was the meeting place of some of the world's great roads. The great trade route from the far off Euphrates reached Ephesus by way of Colosse and Laodicaea and the wealth of the east poured into its markets. The road from Galatia and north Asia came in by way of Sardis. And there was a road from the south which brought into Ephesus the trade of the Maeander valley. It had been called "The Treasure House of Asia," and, as one scholar has pointed out, John may well have been thinking of the glittering markets of Ephesus when he wrote his wonderful description of the merchandise of men, "The cargo of gold, silver, jewels and pearls, fine linen, purple, silk and scarlet, all kinds of scented wood, all articles of ivory, all articles of costly wood, bronze, iron and marble, cinnamon, spice, incense, myrrh, frankincense, wine, oil, fine flour and wheat, cattle and sheep, horses and chariots, and slaves, that is, human souls." (Revelation 18:12, 13). It is fitting that Ephesus has been called "The Vanity Fair of Asia Minor."

The assize town

Ephesus was not only a great trade centre, it was an important political centre as well. First, it was a free city. Scattered throughout the Roman Empire were free cities. They were either cities of ancient fame or cities which had always chosen the right side in the many civil wars. For their fame or for their loyalty they were given certain rights. No Roman garrison was ever quartered in them. They never had the indignity of seeing the Roman eagles marched through their streets. They were self-governing and had even the power of inflicting the death penalty on their own citizens. They had their own laws, their own customs and their own magistrates.

Ephesus had a board of principal magistrates called the Strategoi. It had an elected senate called the Boulé. And it had an assembly of all her citizens called the Demos or the Ecclesia. Of one of its magistrates we read in Acts 19:35. He was the man who pacified the crowd who were so hostile to the Christians, and the Revised Standard Version calls him the Town Clerk. The title scarcely does him justice. He was the keeper of the archives and the public records; in the senate he read and introduced the principal business; and it was he to whom all letters and communications to Ephesus were addressed. The citizens of Ephesus had their own independence and their own political freedom and in that freedom they gloried and rejoiced.

Second, Ephesus was an assize town, the seat of the Roman governor, the proconsul. The Roman governors made tours of their provinces and at certain centres legal cases were heard. To these towns came the Roman judges with their suites and their interpreters, for even in the Greek-speaking world law cases were conducted in Latin. So at certain seasons of the year Ephesus saw all the pomp and panoply of Roman law in action.

The Pan-Ionian games

The month of May was sacred to the goddess Artemis and was actually called Artemision. In that month a great festival was held. There was music and there were gymnastics and there were great games like the Olympic games and into the city crowded nearly the whole population of Ionia to take part. Public spirited men counted it a great honour to have the task of making all the many arrangements that were needed for these games and of counted it a privilege to bear the expenses. These men were given the title Asiarchs, which means "Chiefs of Asia". They are referred to in Acts 19:31. To be an Asiarch was the summit of a man's career. So there were times when Ephesus was crowded to capacity with hordes of people from all over Ionia who had come to the games.

The Temple of Diana

Greatest of the glories of Ephesus was the Temple of Diana which was one of the seven wonders of the world. There had been at least three temples on that site. Away back in the days before history there had been one. Then later all the cities of Asia, helped by Croesus the king of Lydia, the richest man who ever lived, united to build another and it was the glory of the city. But on the very night that Alexander the Great was born, a queer madman called Herostratus set fire to it and burned it down because that was the only way he could think of to get his name into the history books. From the ruins there arose a new and even greater temple which took more than two centuries to build. The Greeks had a saying, "The sun sees nothing finer in his course than Diana's temple." When it was building, the women of Ephesus gave even their bracelets and their necklaces and their jewels to make ornaments for it. Alexander the Great offered all the spoils of his eastern campaign if his name might be inscribed upon it; but the offer was refused for none but the name of Ephesus herself might appear upon the temple.

It was 435 feet long by 220 feet wide by 60 feet high. That is a colossal size; but it must be remembered that ancient temples were not roofed in. Only the central shrine was roofed and the outer parts were lovely colonnades and porticos. Within the colonnades were 127 pillars, each of them the gift of a king. The columns themselves were made of glittering Parian marble and 36 were richly inlaid with gilt and covered with delicate work. The great folding doors were made of cypress and the roof of cedar wood. The stairway to the roof was said to have been cut from one gigantic vine from the island of Cyprus.

In the inner shrine stood the great altar carved by Praxiteles, the greatest of all Greek sculptors, and behind it the great draped velvet curtains. Behind the curtains was the sacred image of Diana. It was one of the half dozen most sacred images in all the ancient world. It was so old that no man knew whence it had come and the belief was that it had fallen from heaven itself. There was even some argument as to what it was made of. Some said cypress, some cedar, some ebony, some vinewood and some stone. To see it would give most of us a shock. We think of Diana as one of the loveliest of Greek goddesses. We speak of Diana "the huntress chaste and fair." But the image was a squat, black, ugly thing. It was an uncouth female figure covered with breasts, to signify fertility, holding in one hand a trident and in the other a club. There was no beauty there, only repulsive ugliness. Yet to millions of people that unsightly image was the most sacred thing in the world and stood for God.

Behind the image itself was a still more inner shrine. In it people came to deposit their treasure for safe-keeping. It has been said that it was the ancient equivalent of the Bank of England. Certainly the temple of Diana was the richest and the safest bank in the ancient world.

The priests were called Megabyzi and were eunuchs from Phrygia. In addition there were thousands of female priestesses with the queer name of Melissae, which means the bees. And in addition to them there were thousands of slaves who swept and tended the precincts of the temple. The Greek word for a temple-sweeper is "Neokoros." Originally it described the humblest and most servile duty in the temple courts; but Ephesus, the great city, was proud to inscibe upon her coins, as her greatest claim to honour, that she was the Neokoros of the Temple of Diana.

The worship was a weird, ecstatic, hysterical business. To shouts and cries and wailings, burnings of incense and playing on the flute, the worshippers worked themselves into an emotional passion, in which nameless and shameless things might happen.

The home of criminals

So far we have been thinking of the greatness of Ephesus. She was a great commercial town; she was a free city; she was an assize town; she was the home of the Pan-Ionian Games; she had the Temple of Diana which was one of the seven wonders of the world. But there was another side to it. She was notoriously a wicked city. The Greeks themselves used to say that every single individual in Ephesus deserved to be throttled one by one. One of the most famous Greek philosophers was called Heracleitus. He was a gloomy soul who was known as the weeping philosopher; and the story ran that when he was asked why he wept, he answered, "What else can I do when I look at Ephesus?"

One of the main reasons for the wickedness of Ephesus was that the temple of Diana possessed the right of asylum. That is to say, if a man who had committed a crime could reach the precincts of the temple, the law could not touch him and he was safe. Legend has it that when the temple was completed Mithradates stood on its roof and declared that this right of asylum should extend all round the temple as far as he could shoot an arrow. He shot and the arrow miraculously carried two hundred and twenty yards. So all round the temple of Diana there was an area where the scum of Asia Minor collected, till the place that was supposed to be sacred was the very centre of a cesspool of iniquity.

Ephesian letters

One other trade Ephesus had; she was the centre of the trade in Ephesian letters. These letters were charms. If a person wanted safe journeyings on a voyage, if a woman wanted a child, if a person wanted an undertaking to have a successful issue, he or she came to Ephesus and bought and wore one of these charms which were supposed, with their mystic, unintelligible words, to be the most powerful in all the world. There was a Greek story of a wrestler who was invincible at the games and who threw every opponent who could be found for him. It was discovered that he was wearing an Ephesian charm round his ankle and when that was taken off his victories ceased at once! Into Ephesus there poured hordes of credulous folk, so that in a superstitious world she was the most superstitious of cities.

Paul at Ephesus

It was there that Paul lived and worked for longer than he did in any other town. He began, as he always did, in the Jewish synagogue. But when he had given the Jews the chance he always gave them, he took the gospel to the city at large. He hired a lecture room and there preached of Christ. The results were sensational. Very briefly the story is told in Acts 19. Wave upon wave of the gospel went out until the whole of Asia had heard of Christ. And then things started to happen. One of the chief industries of Ephesus was the making of little replicas of the temple. These were taken home by the pilgrims, who came from all over, as souvenirs of their visit to Ephesus. The manufacturers of these models suddenly found that their trade was drying up. Christ had so triumphed that Diana was being swept from the field.

Two things were touched—the pride of the people in their temple; and their pockets. The result was an infuriated mass meeting in the city theatre. It was only with difficulty that Paul was stopped from addressing that meeting which would assuredly have lynched him. Paul always believed in looking a mob in the face. It was only with difficulty that the town clerk pacified this hysterical assembly by reminding them that Rome would stand much but not civil disorder. Finally the meeting broke up, but the damage was done and once more Paul had to move on to other spheres.

It is strange how history repeats itself. Almost a hundred years later there was a governor of Bithynia, a neighbouring province, whose name was Pliny. He was very friendly with the Emperor Trajan and used to take all his problems to him. We still have the letters Pliny wrote and the answers Trajan sent. One of Pliny's problems was the Christians. The trouble was that the temples were empty; the traders who had supplied animals for the sacrifices and fodder to feed them were going bankrupt; and as in Ephesus the Christians had to suffer. There are always

those who care for money more than they care for the truth of
God.

It's hard to be a Christian

Sometimes we think that it is hard nowadays to be a Christian.
When we think of that let us think of Ephesus. Here was a city
immersed in trade and commerce and steeped in luxury, the seat
of government of a suspicious power, the centre of pagan
religion, a hotbed of vice and the refuge of criminals, impreg-
nated with superstition, and yet in that very city Paul won
some of his greatest triumphs for Christ. When a general has a
hard job to do he gives it to his best soldiers. There was a great
Spanish mystic who prayed for his people, "May God deny you
peace and give you glory." Things may be hard now but when
we think of Ephesus we should be ashamed of our fears and our
complaints.

CHAPTER EIGHTEEN

The Gathering Storm

The last act

We are coming very near to the last act of the drama of Paul's life. There was never such a traveller as he and yet he was at heart a Jew and dearest of all cities to him was Jerusalem. So he decided that the time had come to go home but he was not going empty handed. The Church at Jerusalem was always poor, and Paul had worked out a plan whereby his new churches might send a gift to it. We find various references to that gift in 1 Corinthians 16:1ff.; 2 Corinthians 9:1ff.; Romans 15:25, 26. Throughout the Churches of Macedonia and of Corinth he had organised a collection the proceeds of which he proposed to carry to Jerusalem as a gift to the Church there.

Paul must have had two objects in organising that collection, and they are the same two which are at the back of all the giving the Church asks and all the offerings the Church makes.

First, Paul organised that collection *to stress the unity of the Church*. It was so easy—and is—to think of the Church in terms of the congregation. It would have been so easy for Philippi and Corinth never to see beyond Philippi and Corinth. But the Church is one great whole of which each local congregation is a part. In one of his greatest passages Paul likens the Church to a body (1 Corinthians 12). In that passage he says that if one member suffers then all suffer. So when Paul organised that collection he wanted to make those who gave to it feel that their eyes must go out beyond themselves, that they were part of one great whole, and that each part was responsible for the welfare of the other. It was William Morris who said that he never saw a beggar or a drunk upon the streets but he had a feeling of personal responsibility for him. We are not merely members of a congregation but members of the Church of Christ, and one of the best ways of remembering that is to send gifts to other parts of the Church which are in need.

Second, Paul wanted to teach his churches *the practical nature of Christian charity*. Often he must have told them about the Church at Jerusalem and the hardships it had to bear; and often they must have felt sorry for their brothers in distress; but now Paul was teaching them that it is never enough simply to *feel* sorry but that sympathy must issue in deeds. Someone has said that when we really pity a person "we go mad to help him." It is one of the most serious faults to feel pity and do nothing beyond feel it. When Paul organised that collection, he wanted to teach those friends of his that Christian charity is a thing of deeds and not of feeling only.

In perils oft

No sooner did Paul prepare to set out for Jerusalem than the clouds began to gather round him; and it became increasingly clear that he was journeying not only to Jerusalem but also to death. He had made his final tour of Macedonia and it is very likely that he was about to sail from Corinth when it was discovered that there was a plot of the Jews against his life (Acts 20:1–3). It was the Passover season; the ships would be crammed with Jews returning to Jerusalem to keep the most sacred of their feasts, for every Jew all over the world prayed then (and still) that he might keep the next Passover in Jerusalem. Perhaps the plot was that on the crowded ship Paul would be silently despatched overboard and never heard of again. The Jews hated him because he had taken what they considered the privileges God had given them and them alone and had opened them to the accursed Gentiles. They would go to any lengths to stop him.

Farewell at Ephesus

No one knew the dangers which lay in front of him better than Paul himself. He delayed his journey but ultimately went on. The ship touched at Miletus which was near to Ephesus. Paul had worked longer in Ephesus than in any other city and he sent for the elders of Ephesus to come to him that he might say good-bye. We can read what he said to them in Acts 20: 17–35. He spoke lovingly of the work he had done among them; he reminded them of their duty as shepherds of the flock of Christ; and he said to them that he was going to Jerusalem and did not know what would happen there. He knew only that dangers and sufferings lay ahead and he was very sure that they would see his face no more (Acts 20:22–25). He had literally to tear himself away from them so unwilling were they to let him go.

Warning at Tyre

So Paul embarked again. The ship was due to unload cargo at Tyre and there Paul sought out the Christians. They warned him that he must not go to Jerusalem if he valued his life, but Paul loved loyalty more than life and went on (Acts 21:3, 4).

Pleadings at Caesarea

On to Caesarea he went and there he stayed with Philip who had been one of the Seven. When Paul was there, a prophet named Agabus came down from Jerusalem. He took Paul's girdle and bound up his hands and feet and then he said to him, "So shall the Jews at Jerusalem bind the man who owns this girdle and deliver him into the hands of the Gentiles." Thereupon all the company besought Paul not to go. But he gave his great-hearted answer, "I am ready not only to be imprisoned but even to die at Jerusalem for the name of the Lord Jesus" (Acts 21: 8–13).

The highest courage

There are two kinds of courage. There is the courage of the man who does a brave thing in the heat of the moment, when he has no time to stop and think of what the consequences may be. And there is a higher courage—the courage of the man who has plenty of time to think, who knows only too clearly the consequences of the thing he is setting out to do, and who yet inflexibly goes on. No matter what people said to Paul, no matter what dangers he himself saw looming ahead, his decision was for going on.

Stratagem in Jerusalem

So Paul came to Jerusalem. In the whole story there is a tragic lack of warmth and of welcome. We know that Paul brought the collection with him from his churches; it is not recorded that the Christians at Jerusalem breathed one word of thanks. Paul told to James and the brethren all that he had done and they glorified God that men from every nation had been swept into the fold of Christ.

But they were worried. They told Paul that there were thousands and thousands of Jews who looked on him as a renegade and a traitor and who slandered him by saying that he encouraged everyone to break the law. They were sure that soon all these Jews would hear of Paul's arrival in the city, that they would recognise him as soon as he walked the streets and that they would raise the most hostile demonstrations against him. So they had a plan.

There were four men who had taken upon themselves the Nazirite vow. If a Jew had been saved from some great peril or delivered from some great sickness, or if he wanted in a special way to show his self-dedication to God, he took this vow upon himself. He bound himself, very likely for a period of thirty days, not to eat meat and not to drink wine and not to cut his hair. It seems that he had to spend the last week actually in the temple premises and when the thirty days were over he had to offer an unblemished year-old lamb for a sin offering, an unblemished ram for a peace offering, a basket of unleavened bread, cakes of fine flour mingled with oil, and a cereal offering and a drink offering. He had then to shave his head and the shaven hair must be burned on the altar with the sacrifice. The regulations are in Numbers 6. Clearly this would be an extremely expensive business and one quite impossible for a poor man to perform. It was therefore looked on as a specially pious and creditable action for some wealthy man to defray the expenses when some poor person took this vow.

The leaders of the Jerusalem Church said to Paul that if he would defray the expenses of those four men who were taking the Nazirite vow and if he would company in the temple with them, that would be a demonstration to the narrower and more rigid Jews that he was not a lawbreaker and an impious person, and much trouble and possible disturbance would be avoided. It must have gone sorely against Paul's grain to do it and yet he agreed (Acts 21:20-26).

Riot in the Temple

The seven days of the final part of the vow had almost passed and things were quiet—then the storm broke. The Temple was composed of a series of areas each more holy than the one which went before. These were successively, The Court of the Gentiles, The Court of the Women, The Court of the Israelites, The Court of the Priests and, finally, the most sacred of all places, The Holy of Holies. No Gentile was allowed to pass beyond the outermost court on pain of death. Between the outer court and the Court of the Women there was a low barrier with inscribed stones which said, "No alien must set foot within this enclosure on pain of death." Even when the Jews were under Roman sway, the Romans allowed them the right to execute any Gentile who broke this inviolable law.

Paul was in the second court because it seems that in it were the little cells in which those who were performing the Nazirite vow stayed for the last week. Into the Temple came certain Jews from Ephesus. Whether by unthinking haste or by deliberate malice they leaped to a certain conclusion. They had seen Paul in the streets with Trophimus, a Gentile Christian from Ephesus, and they knew that Trophimus was one of Paul's comrades. They jumped to the quite wrong conclusion that not only had Paul walked in the streets with Trophimus but that he had brought him beyond that barrier across which no Gentile might step. They were sure that Paul had polluted the Temple with the presence of a Gentile. Immediately they raised a hue and cry; the whole city rushed together in one vast mob; they had but one idea—to lynch Paul; they dragged him out of the inner court and were well on the way to murdering him (Acts 21:27–30).

The strong hand of Rome

But the inflamed Jews had forgotten the strong impartial hand of Rome. In the north-west corner of the Temple area stood the Tower of Antonia which was the Roman barracks. It overlooked the Temple area and there were Roman legionaries ever on guard, for disturbances were always too liable to happen. The guards saw the milling mob below. Down came the commanding officer with a platoon of soldiers. The Jews shrank back for it was dawning on them, through the mists of anger, that they had gone too far.

More for his safety than for anything else, the commanding officer ordered Paul to be chained to two Roman soldiers and started to make his way to the stairway leading to the safety of the tower. He demanded what crime Paul had committed but all that answered him was a confused babel of voices. The crowd began to press in upon them so that they were hardly able to force a way through. Then Paul, in truth at that moment Paul the dauntless, made an amazing request. "May I speak to them?"he said. The commanding officer was amazed for in the uproar he had jumped to the conclusion that Paul was a well-known Egyptian revolutionary and he had not thought that he could speak Greek at all. He gave his consent and Paul, true to his lifelong policy, once again looked the mob in the face (Acts 27:31–40).

Paul states his commission

Paul began to speak, and spoke, not in the Greek tongue which he had used for so long, but in his native Aramaic; and at the sound of their mother tongue the Jews were quiet. He told them that he was a Jew born in Tarsus; that he had been trained by Gamaliel, the greatest of the Rabbis; that once he had been a savage persecutor of the Christians. He told them how he had been on the way to Damascus to root out Christianity and how Jesus Christ had met him on the way. He told them of his blindness and how he had been healed and baptised by Ananias, him-

I

self a devout observer of the law. So far there had been silence, for Paul was an orator and could tell a story.

He went on. He told how he had been in the Temple praying and a vision had come to him and sent him out of Jerusalem to preach his gospel somewhere else. Then he came to the final command of God, "I will send you far away to the Gentiles." Immediately pandemonium broke loose. Here was the plain statement that Paul had taken God's word to Gentiles who were accursed and who had no right to have it. In the eyes of the Jews there was nothing for him but death. And for the commanding officer, there was nothing left but to lock Paul safely in prison that the riot might subside.

I must do it

There is a passage in the writings of John Bunyan in which he tells of his feelings when he had to choose between being true to his faith and facing all kinds of threats and giving up his faith and finding safety. He thought of his wife and children, especially of his little blind daughter whom he loved more than any of the others. "I felt," he said, "like a man who was pulling down his house on the top of himself and his wife and his children. *Yet thought I, I must do it. I must do it.*"

Paul knew what he was facing when he came to Jerusalem; he knew what he was facing when he confronted that mob; yet he, like Bunyan, said to himself, "For the sake of Christ, I must do it." To be true to Christ is worth any suffering in the end.

CHAPTER NINETEEN

Before Governors and Kings for My Sake

Paul the Roman citizen

It was for Paul's own sake that the Roman commander-in-chief arrested him, for it was the strange fact that, for Paul, the only safe place in all Jerusalem was the Roman prison in the Tower of Antonia. But the Roman soldier was worried. He was responsible for the good order of Jerusalem and that was no small task; he knew well that the one thing Rome could not and would not forgive was civil disorder and that therefore this matter must be dealt with with a strong hand. So, to find out the facts of the case, he determined to examine Paul under torture.

He directed that he should be examined by scourging (Acts 22:24). Now before this, in Philippi, Paul had been beaten by the lictors' rods but scourging was very different. The scourge was a long strip of leather, studded here and there with pieces of sharpened bone and weighted with lead. Sometimes, by accident or even design, a criminal under scourging was struck across the face and the blow might blind him by tearing out an eye. Almost always men fainted under the lash; sometimes they went mad and sometimes they died; and, even if they survived the actual scourging, they frequently died from the nervous and physical exhaustion of that dreadful ordeal.

Paul was actually bound, with his back bent to receive the lash, when he quietly but very effectively intervened. "Is it lawful," he asked, "for you to scourge a man who is a Roman citizen and uncondemned?" That was a bombshell. The centurion in charge reported to the commanding officer, Lysias, who was shocked to find that Paul was not only a Roman citizen but that he had been born free, which was more than he had been himself.

Lysias was thoroughly alarmed. He knew for one thing that Paul would never have made this claim falsely, because the penalty for falsely claiming citizenship was in certain cases nothing less than death. And for another thing he knew that he himself had been guilty of two grave errors. First, to scourge a Roman citizen was crime of the first magnitude. Had he done that he would certainly have been dismissed from his post and might even have been executed. Second, it was a breach of the law to scourge anyone without previous examination. It was only when a man refused to speak under normal examination that scourging was allowed at all. So Lysias found himself in an extremely awkward position.

Before the Sanhedrin

It was clear to the commanding officer that, whatever else Paul was guilty of, he was not guilty of any crime against Roman law. It seemed to him that the matter was one for the Jewish courts to deal with. So on the next day he summoned the Sanhedrin and brought Paul before them. The Sanhedrin was the supreme court of the Jews and had jurisdiction over all Jews throughout the world. When the Jews were under Roman rule the Sanhedrin's rights were limited. It could not, for instance, inflict the death penalty without the case being reviewed by the Roman governor; but in matters of faith and religion it was still supreme. It was composed of seventy members, Scribes and Priests and Rabbis, Pharisees and Sadducees, and the High Priest presided over its deliberations.

So before this court Paul was brought. By this time he felt that he had burned his boats and, far from being conciliatory, he was almost recklessly defiant. "Brethren," he began, "I have lived before God in all good conscience up to this day." By beginning in that way he put himself on an equality with the court which was judging him. The normal beginning was, "Rulers of the people and elders of Israel." But Paul pointedly ignored the address of humble inferiority and bluntly addressed the court as an equal.

The presiding High Priest, Ananias, ordered that Paul should be struck across the face. Even amongst the Jews, Ananias was a byword for iniquity. His rapacity for money was famous. He sent armed servants to compel people to give him tithes and he withheld from the humble priests the sustenance they should have had, so that many of them were reduced to starvation. He was one of the best-hated men in all Jerusalem.

In any event he had transgressed Jewish law when he commanded Paul to be struck, for the law said, "He that strikes the cheek of an Israelite strikes, as it were, the glory of God," and again, "He that strikes a man strikes the Holy One." So it is little wonder that Paul blazed out at him. "God shall strike you, you whitewashed-wall," said Paul. "Are you sitting to judge me according to the law, and yet contrary to the law you order me to be struck?" Immediately his accusers charged him with breaking the law by reviling the High Priest. And back came Paul's contemptuous answer, "This man the High Priest? I never knew a man like this could be the High Priest of God" (Acts 23:1–5).

Paul had long since abandoned any hope of obtaining justice or a fair hearing. He now proceeded to fling a kind of intellectual hand grenade into the Sanhedrin's discussion. In the Sanhedrin, as we have seen, there were many interests represented but the two great parties were the Pharisees and the Sadducees. Now these two parties were opposed on many things but in particular there was this difference between them. The Pharisees believed in a life after death and the Sadducees did not. So Paul, in a quite deliberate attempt to disrupt the whole meeting, said, "I am a Pharisee and the son of Pharisees." This was quite true. Then he went on to add, "With respect to the hope and the resurrection of the dead I am on trial." He was called in question for a good deal more than that; but the simple statement tore the Sanhedrin in two. Straightway the Pharisees became his ardent temporary supporters and the Sadducees his even more bitter opponents.

The result was that what had begun as a meeting became an uproar and Paul was in serious danger of being torn in pieces by the excited opposing parties, until in the end Lysias had to step in and rescue him by arresting him all over again. Once again

Paul was taken away to prison because in all Jerusalem that was the only place in which he was safe.

The presence of the Lord

It can have been in no happy frame of mind that Paul laid himself down to sleep that night. Humanly speaking, it seemed that he had become caught up in a web of circumstances that could not end in anything but his death. Just then his Lord came to strengthen and encourage him; for in the night-time Jesus came and told him that he had nothing to fear and that as he had borne his witness in Jerusalem he would yet bear his witness in Rome (Acts 23:11).

A Jewish stratagem foiled

The morning after that unruly meeting, the parties within the Sanhedrin bitterly regretted that their own private quarrel had allowed Paul to slip out of their hands. Then more than forty of the Jews formed a murderous plan. Jewish law laid it down that under certain circumstances murder was justified. If a man was a public danger to life and morals, it was right to remove him. So these forty-odd men bound themselves by a vow that they would neither eat nor drink until they had eliminated Paul. Such a vow was called a *cherem*.

Their plan was this. They asked the Sanhedrin to have Paul brought again before them for examination and they undertook that he would never reach the court alive but would be assassinated on the way. The plan might well have worked but Paul's nephew got to know about it and told him. Paul arranged to see Lysias and the treacherous plot was frustrated (Acts 23:12–22).

To Caesarea

By this time Lysias had had enough. Had all this happened anywhere else, beyond a doubt Paul would have been set free. But Lysias had a problem. Of all cities in the world Jerusalem was the most explosive. Lysias knew quite well that in justice he ought to release Paul; but he also knew quite well that if he did, there was no saying what the consequences might be. There might well be an insurrection which would spread like a forest fire and involve the whole country.

Jerusalem was not the seat of the Roman government in Palestine; the residence of the governor was in Caesarea. Caesarea had the strangest history. Fifty years before the time of Paul it was only a landing place with a single castle called Strato's Tower. But Herod the Great had a passion for building, and he produced in Caesarea an entirely artificial city. He built a great breakwater to make a harbour where any ship could ride at anchor. He filled the new town with stately buildings and palaces in honour of Augustus Caesar and so, although a Jewish king had built it, Caesarea was to all intents and purposes a Hellenistic town.

It was there that the Roman governor had his headquarters. And Lysias, knowing that things had got beyond him, decided to send Paul to Caesarea so that the governor himself might deal with his case. Lysias was taking no risks. The Revised Standard Version has it (Acts 23:23) that he mobilised a force of 470 fighting men to see Paul safely to Caesarea. The figures may really mean that the number was 270 men; but in any event the might of Rome was mobilised to see Paul safely to the governor's judgment seat. With him he sent a letter explaining the circumstances (Acts 23:26–30); and at dead of night Paul set out in the midst of this cavalcade for still another trial.

Lo I am with you

When we think of all this we are bound to wonder how Paul went through with it. The physical and nervous strain must have been almost agonising, especially since Paul was never a completely well man.

On one occasion David Livingstone was in doubt. In front of him stretched a river and on the other side were tribes he knew were hostile. For once in his life he was very nearly for turning back. He took his Bible and it fell open at the last verse of the last chapter of the gospel according to St. Matthew. "Lo," he read, "I am with you alway, even unto the end of the world." "It is the word," said Livingstone, "of a gentleman of the most strict and sacred honour; and there's an end of it." And in the strength of that promise he went on.

It has been said that God never gives a man a task but he gives him the strength to do it. Paul knew that he was not going through with this alone but that Jesus was with him and in that company he went fearlessly and tirelessly on.

CHAPTER TWENTY

I Appeal to Caesar

A Roman governor

So to Caesarea Paul went. The Roman governor at this time was a man called Felix. He had been governor for six years and it was to be another two before he was dismissed from his post.

Felix was a byword for his evil character. He had begun life as a slave. His brother Pallas was favourite of the degenerate Emperor Nero and, by the influence of Pallas, Felix slowly rose to power. First he became a freedman; then he actually rose to be Procurator of Palestine. He was the first slave and freedman in history ever to become the governor of a Roman province. Tacitus, the Roman historian, said of him, "He exercised the prerogatives of a king with the spirit of a slave." It was said that this extraordinary man had actually been married to three princesses one after another. The name of the first is not known. The second was a granddaughter of Antony and Cleopatra. The third, whose name was Drusilla, he had lured away from her husband Aziz by the influence of some magician or fortune-teller.

He was completely unscrupulous. It is true that in turbulent Palestine he had a difficult province to control. But his methods were infamous. There was a famous revolutionary called Eleazar. He succeeded in persuading Eleazar to meet him by the promise of a safe conduct and then he had him murdered. Felix had gained his governorship at least in part by the influence of Jonathan the High Priest. He resented Jonathan's attempt to guide him and to keep him in the right way. He seduced Jonathan's closest friend and persuaded him to contact certain hired thugs. These thugs, with daggers hidden beneath their garments, mingled with the crowd in Jerusalem and succeeded in assassinating Jonathan. They escaped by pretending to look for the murderer and in the search they took the opportunity to carry out a whole series of assassinations.

In the end Felix went too far. In Caesarea there was a long standing argument as to whether the city was Jewish or Hellenistic, and the Jews and the Hellenists were always at daggers drawn. There was an outbreak of mob violence in which the Jews came off best. Felix sent in his troops to support the Gentiles. Thousands of Jews were slain and with Felix's active encouragement the troops sacked and plundered the houses of the wealthiest Jews in the city. In consequence Felix was recalled and only the most strenuous efforts by his brother Pallas saved him from execution. So Felix passed out of history, his name stained with shame.

The Jewish deputation

For all that, Felix was a Roman governor administering Roman law. He sent to the Sanhedrin telling them they must make good their charges against Paul. Any Roman citizen who was arrested must be brought to trial within three days. There was no regulation as to when the trial should end but it must begin in three days. It was five days before the Jewish deputation arrived. Ananias was there with his henchmen but they had employed a Roman pleader called Tertullus to plead their case. He began with the most fulsome flattery of Felix which everyone, including Felix, knew was a complete and nauseating lie. Then he laid his charge against Paul. First, he accused him of being a revolutionary. Second, he accused him of being a Christian. Third, he accused him of defiling the Temple courts (Acts 24:1-9).

Paul began his defence with the simple statement that he was glad that Felix had been long enough in Palestine to understand the life and thought of the country; then he went on without difficulty to rebut the charges made against him (Acts 24:11-21). Felix knew a great deal more about these things than the Jews gave him credit for and for the time being he delayed a decision. But he did give orders that Paul's imprisonment must be made as light as possible and that he should be given every facility to see his friends (Acts 24:22, 23).

Paul and Felix

There must have been an almost irresistible charm about Paul for every Roman official with whom he came in contact dealt most considerately with him. And there was someone else who was interested in Paul. That was Drusilla, Felix's wife. She and Felix came to talk with him. And Paul was not the man to spare them. "He argued about justice and self-control and future judgment." Think of the courage of Paul when every word must have been a rebuke to the guilty couple. (Acts 24:24, 25).

Felix often had talks with Paul. Sometimes he hoped that he would give him a bribe to gain his freedom but Paul was far above that. So for two years his imprisonment dragged on.

There was a Scottish border chieftain who was captured in a raid on England and imprisoned in Carlisle Castle. The little window in the cell was just too high to see out of from the floor. So he used to pull himself up by his hands and look out; and to this day you can see the grooves in the window sill which his hands made as over the years he gazed on the hills which he could no longer roam.

Paul the wanderer must have eaten his heart out in those two years. But we can be certain that the soldiers in Caesarea heard the gospel and that his churches received letters which we no longer possess; and if, as is likely, Luke was with Paul, it may well have been during these two years that he collected the material which he afterwards used to write his gospel.

The coming of Festus

The two years passed and then Felix was recalled. Paul's heart must have leaped for it was a well-known custom for a departing governor to set free those who were in prison at the time of his going, as a final act of clemency. But not Felix. He knew the Jews would be sending a report of his conduct to the Emperor and that it could not but be damaging; and with the intention of conciliating them as far as possible he left Paul in prison. The new governor was Festus. He was a good man but he was faced with a hopeless task in seeking to pacify troubled Palestine and in two years time he died. But to Paul he was just.

I appeal to Caesar

Within three days of his arrival Festus paid a visit to Jerusalem for he wanted to begin by paying the Jewish authorities every respect. Immediately the Jews asked that Paul should be sent to Jerusalem for trial for they had every intention of arranging his assassination on the way (Acts 25:1–3). Festus courteously told them that he was on his way immediately back to Caesarea and that he would deal with the case there. So the Jews came down to Caesarea and levelled all kinds of charges; and Paul stated his innocence. Festus, not knowing the background of the case and willing to conciliate these turbulent Jews, asked Paul if he was willing to go to Jerusalem to stand his trial before the Sanhedrin. Paul knew there would be no justice there and played the last card that he had left, a winning one. "I appeal to Caesar," he said.

It was Roman law that any citizen, if he felt that he was not getting justice in the provincial courts, might appeal direct to the Emperor. If the man was a murderer or a pirate or a bandit caught in the act, that appeal was disallowed; but otherwise the appeal was valid and at once it stopped all local proceedings. Festus took counsel with his assessors; there was nothing to hinder Paul's appeal. "You have appealed to Caesar," said the governor. "To Caesar you go." The die was cast. Nothing could stop Paul's journey to Rome (Acts 25:4–12).

Before a king and queen

But if Festus was to send Paul to Rome, he had to send a report of the case with him and Festus, a just man, did not know quite what to send. In his indecision, distinguished visitors came to see him. Agrippa was the grandson of Herod the Great. Berenice was his sister. The Romans allow him to hold some part of the Jewish Kingdom; in particular he ruled over Galilee and Peraea. It was Agrippa's custom always to pay a state visit to each Roman governor. It was chance which had put him on his throne and chance might just as well put him off again; and he knew that he must omit no courtesy to his Roman masters.

So Agrippa and Berenice came to vist Festus and Festus told

them about Paul. Agrippa said that he would like to see and hear this Paul for himself. Festus readily agreed. What a scene that must have been! Agrippa and Berenice were wearing their purple robes of state; they glittered and glistened with jewels; the thin gold circlet of the royal crown was on their brows. Festus himself, wishing to leave no courtesy undone, had on his scarlet robe of state. All round were the noble friends of Agrippa and Berenice and the governor's suite. In the background stood motionless the tall Roman legionaries, fully accoutred.

Into this scintillating scene entered the little Jewish tentmaker whose name was Paul, his hands in chains; and from the moment of entry it is clear that he dominated them all. Agrippa gave him permission to speak. Paul said that he was glad that he could speak with freedom for he knew that Agrippa would understand. He told of the days of his persecuting time, of the day of days when Jesus Christ stopped him on the Damascus Road, of his commission to the Gentiles, of the Christ who had lived and suffered and died and risen again; and of his desire to take that Christ to all the nations.

Festus had been listening with ever increasing astonishment. The intensity and passion of Paul were plain to see; the atmosphere was electric. Festus had seen Paul's cell littered with books and had seen him poring over them. "Paul," he exclaimed, "you are mad, your great learning is turning you mad." Gently and courteously Paul denied it; then he swung round on Agrippa, "King Agrippa," he said, "do you believe the prophets? I know that you believe." And at this personal appeal Agrippa winced. He did not want this matter pushed home. With an embarrassed laugh and a shrug of the shoulders he said, "In a short time you think to make me a Christian."

To Rome

The spell was broken and the audience was over. Little excited groups of the court were talking. Of one thing they were sure, this man Paul was no criminal. And Agrippa said, "This man could have been set free if he had not appealed to Caesar." But the wheels of official machinery had begun to turn and would not stop till Paul reached Rome and confronted the Emperor himself.

In the presence of the King

We cannot help marvelling at the self-possession of Paul as he faced the King. Latimer was preaching in Westminster Abbey and Henry the Eighth was one of the congregation. Latimer spoke to himself in the pulpit so that all could hear. "Latimer! Latimer! Latimer!" he said, "be careful what you say; the King of England is here." Then there was a long pause and Latimer spoke again. "Latimer! Latimer! Latimer! Be careful what you say; *the King of kings is here*." It was said by the Earl of Morton as he looked down into the grave of John Knox, "Here lies one who feared God so much that he never feared the face of man." Paul's loyalty to the King of kings left him fearless in the face of any earthly king.

CHAPTER TWENTY-ONE

In Peril on the Sea

The last journey

The stage was now set for the last journey Paul ever took. All his life he had been haunted by the desire to see Rome and to preach the gospel there. Someone has called Rome "the great sinful city on the seven hills." Sinful it might be, but it was the centre of the Roman Empire and therefore of the world.

When Paul was in Ephesus, he was planning to go through Greece and Macedonia again, and then comes the sentence, obviously straight from his heart, "After I have been there, I must also see Rome" (Acts 19:21). When he was up against things in Jerusalem and his Lord came to him, the message was, "Take courage, for as you have testified about me at Jerusalem, so you must bear witness also at Rome" (Acts 23:11). When he wrote to his friends in Rome, almost at the beginning of the letter he wrote, "I long to see you, that I may impart to you some spiritual gift to strengthen you." And again, "So I am eager to preach the gospel to you also who are in Rome" (Romans 1:11, 15). At the end of the letter he tells them that he will visit them on his way to Spain; and that when he has taken the collection to Jerusalem he will come to them with joy (Romans 15: 24, 32).

There was no period of his life when Rome was not like a magnet to the heart of Paul; and now he was on his way, a captive in bonds. Doubtless what had always been in his mind was that if he could storm the very heart of the Empire for Christ, the greatest possible step would be taken to winning not only that great city but the whole world. His dream was working out —in God's way, not in his.

True friends

He was put in charge of a centurion called Julius of the Augustan cohort. We do not know for sure just what that cohort was; but perhaps every section of the Roman army had a special Augustan cohort attached to it which carried the despatches to and from Rome and acted as a link between the Emperor and his troops in the field. With Paul were two friends who were friends indeed. One was Luke, the beloved physician, who stayed with him to the very end. The other was Aristarchus, a man from Thessalonica. We may well wonder how it was that a man under arrest was allowed to have two friends with him when he was on his way to trial. If a man could afford it, he was allowed to take two servants or slaves with him when he was travelling under arrest. It may well be that Luke and Aristarchus enrolled themselves as slaves of Paul so that they would not be separated from him but might see things through with him to the very end. Surely friendship could go no further. Paul's friends willingly became his slaves that they might make the last journey with him.

Paul sets sail

It was at Caesarea that Paul embarked. The Roman ships were not as small as we might think. They averaged about fifty tons burthen. But the ships that brought the corn supply from Egypt to Italy were much bigger than that. We know of one, whose name was the "Isis", which was 140 feet long, 36 feet wide and with a draft of 33 feet. She was of no less than 3,250 tons burthen.

They were rather unwieldy vessels. They were the same at the prow and the stern, except that the stern was brought up and bent round like a goose's neck. Usually at the prow they had two great eyes painted, as if the ship had to see her own way across the sea. Often they were called after some god whose image was at the front of the prow like a figurehead. They had no hinged rudder as our ships have, but were steered with two great paddles coming out, one from each side, from the hull near the stern. Usually they had only one mast, to which was attached a great yard-arm with one great square sail made of linen or sometimes of hides stitched together. With all the spread of the canvas on the one mast there was a terrific strain on the timbers of the ship; and the commonest way for a Roman ship to be lost was for her to spring a leak and founder at sea. With the one great square sail these unwieldy ships found it almost impossible to sail into the wind and often had to go long distances out of their true course to find a wind that was suitable. Of course, the Romans had no compasses and no instruments of navigation; so they could sail only when they could see the sun and the stars for it was by them they had to set their course.

When Paul embarked at Caesarea it would be on one of the smaller coasting vessels. Up the coast she went to Sidon to take on more cargo and Julius, the centurion, very kindly let Paul go ashore to visit the Christians there. She was a ship of Adramyttium and no doubt she was bound for there. But at that time of year the Etesian winds blew steadily from the west and all she could do was to creep diagonally across until she passed the north-east tip of Cyprus and then make for the shore. Along the shore there is a current making west and at night the breeze from the land helps, and bit by bit the ship crept her way along to the port of Myra.

A dangerous voyage

At Myra there was one of the great corn ships from Alexandria. We have already seen how big these were. Sometimes they could carry as many as six hundred passengers and had so many sailors that the ship looked like a camp. If we look at the map we will see just how far out of her way this corn ship had got. She was bound from Alexandria to Italy and she had fetched up at Myra. It was the only route she could take while the Etesian winds were blowing.

Paul and the others went on board. Slowly and with infinite difficulty she went along between the mainland and the island of Rhodes, using every little current and every breath of the land breeze at night. When she got the length of Cnidus the correct course would have been to cut due west across the Aegean Sea to Italy but the persistent west wind made that impossible. So she

K

aimed diagonally for Crete, and, passing its most easterly tip, the Cape of Salmone, she came to the little harbour of Fair Havens (Acts 27:1–8).

A storm at sea

So far the voyage had been desperately slow but not dangerous; but by this time anxiety was growing. Acts 27:9 tells us that the fast was already past. The fast was the great Day of Atonement, greatest of all the Jewish days, when the High Priest made atonement for the sins of the people throughout the past year. It came at the end of September. In ancient times sailing was strictly limited after 15th September and was abandoned altogether after 11th November. From then on it was too dangerous to sail.

The corn ship was very late and was cutting things very fine. So they decided that they must abandon the voyage to Rome for that year and seek a harbour in which to lie up for the winter. It is likely that Paul was the most experienced traveller of them all. Prisoner though he was, they sought his advice but when they got it, they did not take it. He told them it was at the peril of their lives that they would go farther. But the master of the ship came to another decision. Fair Havens was not a very secure harbour; there was no sizable town nearby where the crew and the passengers might find relaxation in the winter days. Not far along the coast was a much more commodious harbour called Phoenix and he decided, against Paul's advice, to go and winter there.

The weather flattered only to deceive. At first the south wind took them gently along; and then out of a blue sky came Euroclydon, the dread north-east wind, at more than gale force. There was nothing to do but run before it. There was but one chance. A little to the south of Crete lay the small island of Clauda. If they could only reach its shelter it would give them a short respite to put things in order to face the worst. They made it with difficulty. When everything seemed set fair, the dinghy had been towed behind the ship. Now they had to haul it on board to save its being water-logged or even smashed against the hull.

The tempest rages

By this time the timbers were creaking. The weight of the great sail was splitting the ship and they took steps to frap her. That is to say they took great hawsers and bound them round the ship and hauled them tight as if they were tying up a gigantic parcel ready to burst open. And still the storm raged. There was another terror now. It was possible that the raging north-east wind might blow them on to the Syrtis sands off the north coast of Africa which someone has called "The Goodwin Sands of the Mediterranean." By use of the sail and the rudder paddles they avoided this danger. But the best they could do was to persuade their leaking hulk to drift almost broadside on due west. Everything that could be thrown out was jettisoned from the ship. Even the great yard and the sail went overboard. And all were in terror (Acts 27:9-20).

Paul the leader

It was then that Paul, the natural born leader, took charge. He told them that if they had listened to him this would never have happened; but he also told them that his Lord had spoken to him and he knew that all would be saved and that he himself would yet stand before Caesar. At the same time he also warned them that first they would be shipwrecked. For fourteen days the ship drifted helplessly. It drifted more than 450 miles due west while that storm raged. Then, on the fourteenth night, the sailors knew that land was near because they heard the crash of breakers. When they sounded, the water grew shallower and shallower. There was only one thing to do; the drift of the ship must be stopped and they threw out four anchors from the stern. Then they prayed for morning. It was then that the sailors tried to make a getaway and leave the others to their fate. On the pretext of putting out another anchor, they tried to launch the dinghy. Paul saw it. "These men must stay," he said. "We must all be saved or all perish." As if Paul had been the commanding officer, the soldiers did not hesitate. They cut the ropes which supported the dinghy and let her go. Now none could leave the others (Acts 27:21-32).

The morning comes

When morning came Paul persuaded them all to take some food. They must be fit to face whatever lay ahead. So the two hundred and seventy-six souls on that ship took what might well have been their last meal and commended their souls to their gods. They then emptied the ship of her cargo of wheat so that she would ride as high as possible in the water. There was but one chance; they must run the ship ashore and beach her. As they ran in, they struck a reef. Fortunately they did not strike the rock but the soft clay and now it was each man for himself. The soldiers, remembering that, if any prisoner escaped, they themselves must bear his penalty, were all for butchering the prisoners in cold blood, but Julius, the centurion, had by this time come to admire and respect Pul so much that he forbade it. So those who could swim plunged into the sea while the others got hold of such odd pieces of wood as they could; and in an all but miraculous way all got safe to land.

The greatness of Paul

There are two things in this thrilling story of Paul that we cannot fail to see. The first is that in the darkest and most dangerous hour his fellow voyagers accepted him as their leader. He was under arrest. As far as they knew he was a criminal on his way to trial in Rome. But everyone, even Julius, the centurion, and the Roman soldiers, recognised in him a leader of men. In the last analysis there are only two kinds of people; there are the people who are mastered by their circumstances and there are those who are masters of their circumstances. There are the people who have always to lean on someone else and the people on whom others can lean. Later, when in prison in Rome and writing to his old friends at Philippi, Paul said, "I can do all things *through Christ who strengthens me*" (Philippians 4:13). Paul was one of those people who are masters of all circumstances because they meet them not in their own strength but in the strength of Jesus Christ.

The second thing is that all through that terrible storm and shipwreck he was never afraid. There was a famous English sailor called Sir Humphrey Gilbert. He was on a voyage of exploration and had sailed so far into the unknown that his sailors were terrified. They told him frankly of their fears; they said that they had come so far into the unknown that they felt that even God had forgotten them. Sir Humphrey said to them, "I am as near to God by sea as ever I was on land." Wherever he went he knew that nothing could separate him from God. Paul was like that.

CHAPTER TWENTY-TWO

Journey's End

The last stage

It was in the mercy of God that it was upon Malta that Paul and his company were shipwrecked. There was many a shore where the inhabitants waited ghoulishly for shipwrecks and murdered shipwrecked mariners in order to gain their possessions and to get as their own the cargo of the wrecked ship. But in Malta the people were kind, and Paul and his company stayed there for three months until the sailing time came round again (Acts 28:1–10). It so happened that another of the Alexandrian corn-ships, the "Twin Brothers" (or "Castor and Pollux"), had also wintered in Malta and Julius, the centurion, arranged that he and his charges should get a passage on her to Italy.

Their first port of call was Syracuse in Sicily. There they waited for three days and then sailed on to Rhegium. The narrows between Sicily and Italy gave very little room for the great unwieldy corn-ships to manoeuvre, but when they had waited for one day, the south wind blew and they were able to set sail for Puteoli, the port of Italy where all corn-ships had their terminus. It seemed that the weather which had delayed them for so many months was now eager to hasten them to their destination. It is 182 miles from Rhegium to Puteoli but, with the wind set fair, they made it the next day.

The path ahead

At that moment there must have been tremors even in the heart of Paul. As they sailed into the bay, there to the north lay Lisenum. One of Rome's two fleets was stationed there and Paul must have seen the warships riding at anchor and felt again the sheer might of Rome. On one side of the bay lay Baiae, which someone has called the Brighton of ancient Rome. As Paul saw in the distance the crowded beaches and the coloured sails of the yachts of the rich Romans he must have wondered what chance he had, a little unknown Jewish tentmaker, in face of all the wealth and aristocracy of Rome. And there ahead lay Puteoli. Someone has called that city the Liverpool of Italy; and as Paul saw the quays and storehouses and thronging streets, he must have wondered what would happen to him when he was caught up in this vortex which was Rome. All through the voyage Julius had been considerate and he allowed a week's delay for rest and refreshment at Puteoli. Christians were there, too, and Paul met with them and in their fellowship his heart must have been lifted up.

Nero, the Roman Emperor

Perhaps then for the first time there came home to Paul the thought of the man before whom he was to stand his trial. The name Nero has become a synonym for all that is evil, and deservedly so. He began with a bad inheritance. He was the son of Agrippina and of Cnaeus Dominius Ahenobarbus. When Nero was born, his friends congratulated Ahenobarbus on the birth of a son. He answered cynically that any son born to himself and to Agrippina could not turn out other than a public danger and a universal detestation. When Nero was three years old, his mother was banished as a political danger. The child was left with an aunt who handed him over to two slaves, the one a barber and the other a dancer, to educate. What a childhood for a future Emperor! When Agrippina's uncle Claudius came to the imperial throne, she was brought home and given back her honour and her position. She had but one dream now, that some day Nero might be Emperor. Fortune-tellers used to warn her that if ever that happened, Nero would kill her, his own mother; and she would answer, "Let him kill me, so long as he reigns as Emperor."

But there was a long way to go. Agrippina took the first step. Although Claudius was her own uncle, she persuaded him to

marry her. Claudius already had two children, a son called
Britannicus and a daughter called Octavia. Octavia was betrothed
to a brilliant young Roman called Lucius Julius Silanus. Agrippina managed to get him accused of a crime that he had never
committed and he was driven to suicide. She then procured
Nero's betrothal to Octavia. Step by step she was working out
her plan.

By sheer persistence she persuaded the weak-minded Claudius
to adopt Nero as his son and Nero, being three years older than
Britannicus, was now in direct line for the throne. But first of all
Claudius must be eliminated. There was a famous woman
poisoner in prison at the time called Locusta. Agrippina first
seduced Halotus, who tasted all Claudius' food before his master
ate it, and Xenophon, Claudius' doctor, from their loyalty. She
then produced from Locusta a poison which she put into a dish
of Claudius' favourite mushrooms. The Emperor was too slow
in dying and Xenophon hastened his end by tickling his throat
with a poisoned feather.

With a coup d'état of breathtaking audacity, Nero was pro-
claimed Emperor. For a time things went well. For five years
Rome was never better governed, for Nero left things to Seneca,
the great philosopher, and to Burrus, the great general, and men
looked back on that five years as a golden age. But the breach
between Nero and his mother was widening and Nero began to
become a murderer in his own right.

Britannicus was ever a danger and Nero disposed of him in the
subtlest way. A draught was prepared for him. His taster tasted
it and found it harmless but it was too hot to drink with comfort.
Britannicus asked for water to cool it; the poison was in the
water and, when he poured it into the draught and drank, he fell
dead. Still the tension was growing between Agrippina, the
murderess, and Nero whom she had taught to be a murderer. In
the end Nero turned on her. He arranged that she should be taken
for a sail off Baiae, with all the pomp and panoply of a queen, but
the boat was constructed to disintegrate in the water. Almost
miraculously she escaped. A freedman called Anicetus was com-
missioned to murder her in cold blood. As he came into her room,

where she was alone with one slave girl, she knew why he had come and drawing aside her robe, she said, "Strike my womb; it bore a Nero."

The crimes of Nero make him one of the worst criminals in history. He arranged the murder of Octavia; he kicked his second wife Poppaea to death when she was expecting a child. He set fire to Rome until the city burned for seven days and nights and the citizens were united in a hopeless "bond of misery." He blamed the fire on the Christians and tortured them by rolling them in pitch, setting them alight and using them as living torches in his garden; or by sewing them in the skins of wild animals and setting savage hunting dogs to tear them to pieces. There is scarcely a crime in the calendar which Nero did not commit.

Many of these crimes were still to come when Paul set foot on the quay at Puteoli; but even then all men knew what Nero was, and it was he who was to try Paul's case. If ever Paul needed his courage it was now.

The road to Rome

So they set off for Rome. They were aiming for the Appian Way. That was the great road that led from Rome to Brindisi and which carried all the traffic that would cross the Adriatic to Dyrrachium and take up the Egnatian Road there for the East. The road from Puteoli joined the Appian Way at Capua and then on to Apii Forum. Apii Forum was a place where horses were changed and was a rough and disorderly town.

Then things began to happen. The progress of Paul became less that of a criminal than of a king. The Christians from Rome came to meet him. They had never seen him before but they came to welcome him like an Emperor coming home. On they went to the town called the Three Taverns, where the cross-road from Antium joined the Appian Way; and there still more Christians came to meet Paul. When he saw them he thanked God and took courage (Acts 28:15). Slowly it was being borne in on him again that, come what may, he was one of a great company. The loneliness was gone; now he knew there were many who were holding up his hands with their prayers.

Rome

So Paul came to Rome. He was handed over to the captain of the guard and it must have been with real regret that he said goodbye to the courteous and kindly Julius. But in Rome also Paul was kindly treated for he was allowed to live by himself with a soldier as his guard. A prisoner Paul might be, but he was a missionary to the end. As usual he began with the Jews but they received him chillingly and he had little success (Acts 28:17-29).

Once again he turned to the Gentiles. It is impossible to tell the extent of the work that he achieved in Rome. There was a soldier with him always and it is certain that many of those who came to their guard duty as a time of weary boredom stayed to pray. To his churches he poured out a flood of letters, for even in prison the care of all the churches was on his shoulders.

The story without an end

It is a great regret that we do not know the end of the story. For two years Paul was in captivity. He was allowed to live in his own house but nonetheless he was a captive. Why was the captivity so long? It may well be that the Jews had no real wish to bring him to trial and sought only to postpone the day of his trial. They could plead that they had to procure evidence. They could plead that they must send their agents to Thessalonica and to Philippi, to Corinth and to Ephesus and to many another town to build up their case; and we can easily see how the weeks would turn to months and the months to years and still the case could be put off.

The triumphant ending

We wonder why Luke stops the story of Acts where he does. And yet it stops with what is almost a cry of triumph (Acts 28: 30, 31). Its word is "unhindered." It leaves Paul preaching the gospel in Rome without hindrance. What Luke wanted to show was how Christianity arrived at Rome.

Someone has said that Acts might well be called "How they brought the Good News from Jerusalem to Rome." It begins with a little band of Jewish Christians huddled in a room in

Jerusalem, with the apparently hopeless commandment to go out and win a world for Christ. It ends with city after city stormed for Christ and with Paul at the very centre of the world preaching the name of Jesus. If only Christianity could be firmly planted in the capital of the world its future was certain; and Paul had come to Rome. True he was an ambassador in bonds, but his ambition was realised.

The last scene of all

Let us take one last look at Paul in his captivity. He writes to Timothy (2 Timothy 4). He is lonely because only Luke is with him. The winter is coming on and it is cold; he would like the cloak he left at Troas with Carpus. He wants the books and the parchments. What were they? Perhaps they were the precious rolls of his Hebrew Bible. Perhaps they were the first accounts of the life and teaching of Jesus. Perhaps they were the diplomas of his citizenship which he needed for his trial.

It is strange how history repeats itself. Another hero of the Christian faith was lying in prison. His name was William Tyndale; his crime was that he had given the Bible to Englishmen in the English language; and as he lay awaiting death he wrote to his friends and asked them to send him in prison, "A warmer cap, something to patch my leggings, a woollen shirt, and above all my Hebrew Bible."

But in spite of everything there is no defeat. "I have fought the good fight, I have finished the race, I have kept the faith; Henceforth there is laid up for me the crown of righteousness." Paul has come to the end like a fighter, weary but undefeated; like an athlete exhausted but triumphant; like a standard-bearer, battered but with his standard intact.

CHAPTER TWENTY-THREE

Who is able to do Exceeding Abundantly

The faith of Paul

So far we have been thinking about Paul's life, the journeys he made, the cities he visited, and the people he met. Now we must think about Paul's faith. We must try to see some of the great things he believed and taught to others. We begin at the beginning and ask first, What did Paul believe about God?

One God

With all his heart Paul believed there was only one true God. He was a Jew and he had been brought up in that faith. In Paul's day, as to-day, every Jewish synagogue service began with the repetition of the sentence that is the heart of all Jewish religion, "Hear, O Israel; the Lord our God is one Lord." Paul believed in one God of the whole universe. To many of the people to whom he preached that was a completely new idea because they believed in all sorts of gods. There was Zeus who was the chief of the gods; Mercury who was the messenger of the gods; Poseidon who was the god of the sea and the storms; Hephaestion who was the god of fire and of the trade of the smith; Aphrodite who was the goddess of love. There were hordes of gods and always new ones were being introduced.

The Greeks who really thought about things laughed at all this. Lucian, one of these thinking Greeks, drew a picture of heaven in one of his books and of the hordes of gods who lived there and of the new gods who were seeking admission. He imagined a proclamation going out in heaven to those who were trying to gain entry. "When you are called, you are all to come bringing clear proof and undoubted testimony of your father's and of your mother's name; of why you were made a god and how; of your tribe and of your brotherhood; and whosoever does not bring sufficient proof will no longer be deemed eligible for a seat in the house, no matter how huge his temple upon earth, or how high he may be held in the esteem of mortals."

The cultured Greeks laughed at the whole business; but it was very different for the ordinary people. They lived in terror. There were so many gods that they could never be quite sure that they had not offended one or forgotten the honour he should have had, and so they could never really be happy or free of care.

Paul came with his message that there is only one God of all the universe. The wise Greeks must have felt that this was the very truth that they were seeking; and the common people must have heaved a mighty sigh of relief that at last they could be free from the unknown terrors that had encompassed them.

The Father

To Paul the one God was Father. There is not one of his letters in which he does not call God Father; and always he used that name right at the beginning, as if it was the most important thing about God that he knew. "For us," said Paul, "there is one God, *the Father*." This again was quite new to the people to whom he preached. They had thought of God as King and as Judge, but they had never had the lovely thought that he was Father.

Once a Roman Emperor was riding in triumph through the streets of Rome after he had won a great victory. At a certain place on the route was a little platform on which sat the Empress and the Emperor's little son, to see the spectacle. As the procession came opposite, the little boy jumped off the platform, put his head down and burrowed his way through the crowd. He was just about to run out into the middle of the road to meet his father' chariot, when a great, tall Roman legionary, one of the regiment whose men were lining the roadside, caught him and swung him up in his arms. "You can't do that, boy," he said. "Don't you know who is in the chariot there? That's the Emperor himself."

And the little boy laughed down at the soldier. "He may be your Emperor," he said, "but he's my father."

Paul told men of a God who was not distant like a judge or an emperor, but who was the Father of all men.

The creator

To Paul this God who was the only true God and the Father of men, was also the creator of the world. "For from him," said Paul, "and through him, and to him, are all things" (Romans 11:36). Paul was quite sure that he was living in a world made by God. Just because of that the whole world spoke to him of God. He said that through the things we can see we can catch a glimpse of the unseen things that are eternal (Romans 1:19–21).

Later, a great Christian called Tertullian felt just the same about the world. He said, "One flower of the hedge-row by itself—I do not say a flower of the meadows; one shell of any sea you like—I do not say the Red Sea; one feather of a moorfowl—to say nothing of a peacock—will they speak to you of a mean creator?" And again he said most beautifully, "If I offer you a rose, you will not scorn its creator."

When we see the power and the beauty and the bounty of the world, it tells us something of the God who made it. There is nothing which gives greater insight into the character of a man than some bit of workmanship he has produced. The world is God's workmanship and through it we can learn about the God who made it.

God still creating

Paul believed that this God who had created the world was still active in the world, still filling it, as it were, with fresh acts of creation. Paul said, "Neither he who plants nor he who waters is anything, but only God who gives the growth" (1 Corinthians 3:7). Paul had discovered that men can do many things but not create life. Men can make a synthetic seed; it is exactly the same as a natural seed, with the same chemical elements in it, but there is one difference—it will not grow. Paul would have said that every time we see a growing plant or a new life in the world, we see a sign that God is still creating.

God our guide

Paul was sure that God not only created and controlled the world but guided and planned all his life. That same God, who was great enough to hold a world in his hand, was not too great and not too busy to control the life of the individual person. Paul believed that God had a plan for him even before he was born. "God," he said, "had set me apart before I was born" (Galatians 1:15). It was God who called him to be an apostle (Galatians 1:1). Things do not happen just by chance and in a haphazard way. God has a purpose for each one of us. We can be quite sure that no matter who we are we matter to God.

God and the everyday

Paul believed that not only had God a plan for his whole life, but would, if asked it, give him his guidance every day. When writing to his friends at Corinth, he said that he would come to see them soon *if the Lord will* (1 Corinthians 4:19). When he was writing to his friends at Rome he said that he was praying that he might have a prosperous journey, so that, *by God's will*, he might come and see them (Romans 1:10). Paul felt that every moment he was under the guidance of God. He never did a thing, never took a step, without asking God if it was the right thing to do, the right step to take. It is told of a famous Christian statesman that he had a little room built off his study and before he took any great decision he always went into it for a moment or two and asked God's advice. We should always be like that.

A supplying God

Paul believed that God gives not only guidance but also the strength to follow that guidance. "Our sufficiency," said Paul, "is from God" (2 Corinthians 3:5). "My God," he said to his friends at Philippi, "will supply every need of yours" (Philippians 4:19). If anyone who knew where his duty lay had said to Paul, "*I* could never do that," Paul would have answered, "It is not *you* who has got to do it; it is you *and God*."

Paul believed, because he had found it true by experience, that God never gives anyone a task to do without giving him the strength and the help he needs to do it. Once Frank Salisbury, the famous artist, painted a wonderful picture. A fellow artist wrote to congratulate him and in his letter he said, "I congratulate you on the wonderful picture you have painted—or rather *that God has helped you to paint*." Paul knew that all through life God was supplying him with the strength and the courage he needed to do the work that was given him to do.

God the judge

One other thing Paul believed about God—he believed that God was Judge. More than once Paul said that some day we would have to stand before the judgment seat of God and give account for the things we have done in this life (Romans 14:10; 2 Corinthians 5:10). That is why he felt this life was so tremendously important. He felt that all the time we are living here we are either winning or losing the crown God has for us.

A great man, when he was still quite young, was asked why he worked so hard and why he did not allow himself the questionable pleasures other people allowed themselves. He said, "I am quite sure that some day there is going to come to me some big task and I want to make myself ready for it when it comes." Paul felt that all life was like that and wanted himself and all his friends to live in such a way that some day he and they would hear God say, "Well done!"

To Paul, God was the God who made us and the world in which we live, the God who loves us like a Father, the God who guides our lives and who, if we ask him, directs our every action, the God who gives us the strength we need to be true, and the God, before whom, at the end, we shall some day stand—the one true God in life and in death.

CHAPTER TWENTY-FOUR

O Wretched Man That I Am

Paul's idea of man
We have seen what Paul believed about God; now we must look at the other side of the picture and see what he thought about man. A man is bound to take his ideas about man from himself. It is when he examines his own heart and looks at his own struggles and remembers his own failures that he learns about man in general. There is a chapter in Paul's letters which might well be called his spiritual autobiography. That is the seventh chapter of the letter to the Romans. If we read it, we find the tale of Paul's own struggles and we see what he thought about the nature of man. From it we learn one thing straight away— as someone has put it, "Whatever man is, he is not what he was meant to be."

A mixture
Of one thing Paul was sure—that he himself was a quite inexplicable mixture. There was one part of him that wanted to do the right thing, and there was another that wanted to do the wrong. The things he wanted to do he somehow could not do; and the things that he did not want to do he somehow could not help doing. It seemed that inside him there were two opposite principles warring against each other and always keeping his life in an uneasy tension. "I do not do the good I want, but the evil I do not want is what I do."

This experience which tortured Paul is one which comes to everyone. Robert Burns, writing of his own life, once said, "My life reminded me of a ruined temple; what strength, what proportion in some parts; what unsightly gaps, what ruin in others."

Studdert-Kennedy has a poem in which he describes the feelings of an ordinary soldier in the First World War. The public was telling him that he was a hero fighting for his country; but when the chaplain had him at a parade service, he told him he was a miserable sinner.

> "Our padre says I'm a sinner,
>   And John Bull says I'm a saint;
> But they're both of them bound to be liars,
>   For I'm neither of them, I ain't.
> I'm a man and a man's a mixture
>   Right down from his very birth,
> For part of him comes from heaven,
>   And part of him comes from earth.
> There's nothing in man that's perfect;
>   There's nothing that's all complete.
> He's nobbut a great beginning
>   From his head to the soles of his feet."

Everyone has this experience of having two selves. Often when we know what is right we do what is wrong, even when we do not really want to do it. And often when we give in and do the wrong, we hate it all the time we are doing it. Plato said that the soul was like a charioteer, who had to drive two horses yoked to the chariot. The one horse was gentle and biddable; the other was wild and undisciplined. Their names were reason and passion.

Frustration

The inevitable result of this tension was a certain frustration and feeling of helplessness. In those early days Paul had the feeling that, no matter how hard he tried, he just could not live the life he knew he ought to live. A famous man used to have an ever recurring dream. He was in a little green field surrounded on all sides by high walls; and the name of the field was human ability and the name of the walls was human limitation. Paul felt that man was a mixture and that man's life, so long as he remained that way, was frustrated and helpless.

The law

But one might argue, "Man has the law; he has the command-ments and they tell him what to do. Surely with the help the law gives, he can find some satisfactory kind of life." But Paul felt that the law, instead of being a help was a curse. He felt that in two ways the law actually made sin easier instead of harder and so made matters worse.

(*a*) If there was no law, there could be no such thing as sin, because a man did not know what was right and what was wrong. We cannot blame a person for ignorance when he never had the chance to know. There are things a little child may do for which an adult would be punished. We can excuse a savage for doing things that we would condemn in a civilised man. In that sense, if there was no law there would be no sin, and the law has made matters worse.

(*b*) Very often human nature is such that, if a thing is forbidden, that is the very thing we want to do. There is a kind of perversity in each of us which makes us want to do what we are told not to do. With a whole field of grass to graze in the cow sticks her head through the fence to get the grass at the side of the road. Augustine tells us how, as a boy, he and his gang used to steal apples, not because they wanted them, and not because they were good to eat. They were actually sour and unpalatable. They stole them just because "forbidden fruits are sweetest." Paul found that the law actually wakened the desire to sin and so again it made matters worse.

Sin

Paul felt that man was a mixture, that because he was a mixture he was always helpless and frustrated, and that the fact that he possessed the law simply made matters worse. All this is just to say that man is what he is because of sin.

Let us see if we can find out what Paul meant by sin. We will do that most easily by looking at five different words he uses, because each has something to tell us about what sin is.

Missing the mark

The first is the Greek word *hamartia*. This word comes from shooting or aiming at something, and means "a missing of the mark." That means that sin is the failure to be what we ought to be and what we could be. It is easy to look back and to know that we could have done a great deal better than we did. The idea is that God has an ideal for each of us, and we have failed to reach it. First of all, Paul thought of sin as missing the mark.

Going over the line

The second is *parabasis*. This means "a stepping across a line." The idea is that there is a line drawn between right and wrong and deliberately to step across that line is to sin. We often use the phrase ourselves, "I draw the line at that." So Paul thought of sin as stepping across the line which divides right from wrong.

Slipping up

The third is *paraptoma*. The idea of this word is "slipping up." It is not so deliberate as stepping across the line; it is rather, through lack of care, stepping on a slippery place and falling. Paul thought of sin as slipping when, if we had been more careful, we could have walked erect.

Breaking the law

The fourth is *anomia*. The idea of this word is "lawlessness." It means the deliberate breaking of a law which we knew existed and which we knew we ought to keep. It means that we know God's law from his book, from our conscience, from the teaching and example of good and godly people, and yet, in spite of that knowledge, we do what we are commanded not to do. Paul thought of sin as knowing what is right and doing what is wrong.

An unpaid debt

The fifth Greek word for sin is *opheilema*. This literally means "a debt". The idea is that we owe God certain things. Because God is God, and because he has done so much for us, we owe him our love, our loyalty and our obedience; and not to give him these things is to sin. Paul thought of sin as the failure to pay to God the debt we owe him.

The flesh

There is a word which occurs in Paul's letters over and over again in connection with sin; that is "the flesh." In the seventh chapter of Romans he writes at the end, "So then, I of myself serve the law of God with my mind, but with my flesh I serve the law of sin." When Paul spoke of the flesh he did not mean only our bodies. The Greeks had an idea that, when a man was born, two spirits were assigned to him. The one continually invited him to goodness, the other continually invited him to evil; and his whole life depended on which invitation he accepted. The Jews had the idea that in every man there are two natures. There is the good nature which tries to persuade a man always to take the good way; and there is the evil nature which always tries to make a man take the wrong way.

When Paul spoke of the flesh he meant something like that. By the flesh he meant that bit of us which gives a bridgehead to sin, which responds to the invitations of sin, which makes us want to do wrong. There is a bit of us which knows what is right and which wants to do it; that Paul would call our spirit. There is a bit of us which wants to do wrong and is often stronger; it Paul calls the flesh. If we could only get rid of that bit of our nature which wants to do wrong, we would not sin. But by ourselves we cannot. That is what Paul meant when he spoke of the flesh as being the part of us where sin gets its chance. So now we have thought of man and of the disease of sin. In our next chapter we turn to God's cure for that disease.

CHAPTER TWENTY-FIVE

Jesus Christ and Him Crucified

The effect of sin

In the last chapter we saw that man is a mixture of good and bad and that there is always an element of defeatedness in his life; and we saw that the cause of all this was sin. Man had broken God's commandments and gone against his will. Because of this there was a barrier between man and God. When we disobey someone we ought to obey and when we hurt someone we ought to love, there is always a kind of barrier between us and that person, and we are never comfortable in his presence until we have been forgiven. Paul believed with all his heart that it was to take away the barrier between us and God and to put us right with him that Jesus came into the world and lived and died. Paul wanted to tell men about this in ways that they would understand, and so he looked around to get a series of pictures which would help explain what Jesus had done for men.

The picture from the law courts

First of all, Paul went to the law courts and took a picture from there. He said, "Since we are justified by faith, we have peace with God" (Romans 5:1). We must be careful to see what "justified by faith" really means. When we speak of justifying ourselves or of being justified we mean that reasons can be found to prove that we acted rightly. But that is not at all what Paul means. The word he uses means "to treat a person as if he was a just man." It means that God, even when we have done wrong, still treats us and still loves us as if we had done nothing but right.

Once, during the American Civil War, when the southern

states revolted from the Union, someone came to Abraham Lincoln and asked him how he was going to treat those southerners when they were finally conquered and brought to heel. Lincoln's answer was, "I am going to treat them as if they had never been away." That is exactly what justification means. Although we have done wrong, God treats us in his love as if we had never been away.

Jesus had already taught men that God was like that. He told them the story of the Prodigal Son (Luke 15:11–32). When the son made up his mind to come home from the far country, his intention was to begin by saying to his father, "Treat me as one of your hired servants." But his father never gave him the chance to say it. He took him back, not as a servant, but still as a son.

So Paul has this lovely picture of God. He thinks of God as a Judge, but not what we might call "a hanging judge" bent on our punishment and destruction; rather as a Judge who, although we have broken his laws, is still determined in his love to treat us not as criminals but as sons.

The picture from friendship

Paul takes another picture from friendship. He speaks of God who was in Christ reconciling the world to himself (2 Corinthians 5:18–20). He has a picture of two friends who have quarrelled and of someone who brings them together again and restores the harmony that should never have been broken. But Paul never speaks of God being reconciled to us but always of us being reconciled with God. It is not God who has quarrelled with us; it is we who have drifted away from him. Jesus himself said, "Blessed are the peacemakers." He was the greatest peacemaker of all because, when the friendship between man and God had been broken because of man's disobedience, he restored it.

The picture of the freed slave

Paul takes another picture from the strangest place, the slave market. He talks of us being bought with a great price and therefore belonging to God (1 Corinthians 6:20). In Greece there was a rather lovely custom when a slave wanted to become free. Every slave had his price and before he could be free he had to collect the money to pay for his freedom. Sometimes he would scrape and save for years and years. He would do odd jobs for a few coppers, would work early and late to gain a few pence and every penny earned he would take and would deposit in the temple of some god. Finally, when he had saved the money required for his freedom, he would ask his master to go to the temple of the god with him. The priest would come out with the money and tell the master that the god was willing to give him this money if he would sell the slave to him. So the master took the money and the slave became the property of the god, and because he was the property of the god he was free from all men. Now he was no longer a slave; he was no longer even his own; he was the god's man.

Paul says that is a picture of what Jesus did. We were the slaves of sin and Jesus paid the price to set us free, and therefore we belong no longer to ourselves but to him, both body and soul.

The picture from history

For one of his pictures Paul went to the history of his own people. Two thousand years earlier the Israelites had been slaves in the land of Egypt. God had come to their rescue. He had raised up Moses; he had enabled them to escape from Egypt; he had brought them safely through the Red Sea and he had finally guided them to the Promised Land. The Jews never forgot this and had a word they used to describe it again and again. They said, "The Lord has *redeemed* you from the house of bondage" (Deuteronomy 7:8). So Paul speaks of Jesus, "In whom we have redemption, the forgiveness of sins" (Colossians 1:14). Paul felt that, just as the Jews long ago had been slaves to the Egyptians, we are the slaves to sin; and, just as the power of God had brought the Jews out of their slavery, so it was Jesus who redeemed us from slavery to sin.

The picture from the Temple

Paul was a good Jew and he knew all about the Temple and the Temple sacrifices. The Jews believed that, if they gave certain sacrifices to God, these sacrifices won God's forgiveness for their sins. So Paul says of Jesus that God set him forth as an *expiation* for our sins (Romans 3:25). That is a difficult word. But it is just as if he is saying, "All through the ages the sacrifices have been offered in the Temple for the sins of men; but Jesus gave himself as a perfect sacrifice and by his life and by his death he won for us forgiveness for our sins." So he writes of Jesus, "Walk in love, as Christ loved us and gave himself up for us, a fragrant offering and sacrifice to God" (Ephesians 5:2). In a sentence Paul would have said, "He loved us and gave himself for us."

The picture from the accountant's office

Once Paul went to the world of business for a picture of what Jesus did. He said that, because of what Jesus did, God was not counting their trespasses against men (2 Corinthians 5:19). There are really two pictures there. The one is an old, old picture. It was the custom of ancient kings and chiefs to keep a book or roll of their subjects. The book had two lists. One was the list of those who were true, good and loyal subjects. The other was the list of those who were disobedient, rebellious and disloyal and who deserved nothing but punishment. Paul's picture was that our names were on the roll of those who deserved punishment, but, because of what Jesus did, our names were taken from that roll and put on the roll of those the king loved.

But there is another picture. It is the picture of an accountant keeping his books. In the book there is against each man's name a credit or a debit balance. Paul's second picture is that in God's book there is a debit balance against every man's name, for no man has been as good as he ought to be; but through Jesus that balance is wiped out.

He puts this picture in still another way when he is writing to the Colossians. He says (2:14) that Jesus cancelled the bond which stood against us with its legal demands. In Paul's day people wrote their letters and their records on a substance called

M

papyrus. It was quite like brown paper, but it was made from the pith of the bulrush. The ink they used was made of soot and gum and water. It had no acid in it like our ink and therefore the colour did not bite into the paper but simply sat on the top of it, as chalk writing sits on the surface of a blackboard. When people wanted to erase anything, they did not use a rubber or penknife to scrape it out; they simply used a sponge and wiped it off. So Paul says, "There was a charge sheet against each one of us; but Jesus, as it were, took a sponge and wiped out the charges against us."

Thus in different ways Paul uses the picture of a record against us which Jesus cancelled.

The picture from the family

Paul takes one other picture to show what Jesus did for us. This time it is from the family. He speaks of God sending his son that we might receive the *adoption* of sons (Galatians 4:5).

In the ancient world it was quite common for families to adopt. It was a very serious step. If it was a child who was being adopted, the father went through a kind of little play in which he sold his son to the person adopting him, so that the lad would belong entirely to him. If it was a grown man who was to be adopted, he had to go to the highest court in the country. He had to repudiate the gods of his own family and accept the gods of his new family. When a man was adopted, all debts and contracts of his past life were cancelled. He was looked on as being a completely new man, living a completely new life. And as for the future, he was on exactly the same basis as any other son. Nero was no blood relation of Octavia but in the eyes of Roman law he was her brother just as much as if her father, Claudius, who had adopted him had been his real father; and the Roman senate had to pass a special law to allow him to marry her.

Paul felt that God had adopted us because of what Jesus had done. Because of that, we have a completely new life; we are new people; and are in the most real sense sons of God.

The work of Jesus

Paul believed that it was the life and death of Jesus that made all these pictures into realities. Unless Jesus had lived and died, they would have remained lovely pictures. There is the picture of *Justification*. It is true that God treats sinners as if they were good people. But, unless God is untrue to himself, sin must have its punishment and Jesus bore that punishment. There is the picture of *Reconciliation*. It is true that the friendship is restored. But to draw near to God we must have clean hands and a pure heart. It is Jesus who supplies what we have not got ourselves. There is the picture of *Redemption*. Someone has to pay the price of liberating the slave. It is Jesus who pays that price by his life and death. There is the picture of *Expiation*. A perfect sacrifice, is needed. It is Jesus who is himself that sacrifice. There is the picture of *Imputation*. Someone has to pay the debt. It is Jesus who pays it. There is the picture of *Adoption*. A price is paid when a son passes into the possession of his new father. It is Jesus who pays that price.

All of God

There is one thing about which we must be very careful. We must never think of Jesus changing the attitude of God to men; nor of Jesus as being gentle and loving and God as being angry and stern. Behind everything is God. It was God who sent Jesus into the world because he loved us. No one understands it all. But it was something like this. There are two great qualities in God. He is *holy* and because he is holy, sin must be punished. He is *love* and because he is love, sin must be forgiven. So there was nothing for God to do except that his love should in Jesus pay the price of bringing men back to himself. That is why Jesus was for Paul the most important person in the world; that is why Paul could say, "For to me to live is Christ" (Philippians 1:21).

CHAPTER TWENTY-SIX

The Just Shall Live by Faith

The master word

"Faith" was for Paul the master word. If we had asked him what was the greatest thing in the world, he would have answered, "Faith." If we had asked him what was the centre of the Christian religion, he would have answered "Faith." If we had asked him what was utterly essential for a man to be a Christian, he would have answered "Faith."

Fidelity

There is more than one element in Paul's idea of faith. By faith he means *fidelity*. He meant a loyalty to Jesus Christ which nothing could seduce. When he wrote to the Church at Rome, he said that all the world had heard of their faith (Romans 1:8). When he wrote to the Colossians, he spoke of the firmness of their faith in Christ (Colossians 2:5). When he wrote to the people of Thessalonica, he spoke of their steadfastness and their faith (2 Thessalonians 1:4). When he wrote to the Church at Philippi, he spoke of the sacrifice and the service of their faith (Philippians 2:17). When Paul used the word faith in this sense, he meant that unswerving loyalty which keeps a man true to his master in any circumstances, in any danger, in spite of any threat or any opposition.

In the days when the Stewarts were seeking the throne in Scotland, the Marquis of Huntly, called the Cock o' the North, was one of Prince Charlie's men. He was caught by government agents and brought to trial. He was shown the headsman's block and axe, and told that, unless he gave up his loyalty to Prince Charlie, he would be executed there and then. His answer was,

"You can take my head from my shoulders, but you will never take my heart from my king." That is fidelity.

In the second century there was an aged minister in Smyrna called Polycarp. There was a riot, and someone suggested that the Christians should be lynched. The old man was taken and brought before the Roman magistrate. He was told that he must give up being a Christian or be burned at the stake. He answered, "Eighty and six years I have served him and he has done me no wrong. How can I blaspheme my King who saved me?" And he died rather than be disloyal to Jesus. That is fidelity.

If we have this kind of faith it will mean that, no matter what company we are in and no matter what loyalty will cost, we will never be ashamed to show whose we are and whom we serve. Robert Louis Stevenson once wrote a prayer that, through all the chances and the changes of life, down even to the gates of death, God would keep us true to ourselves, true to our loved ones, true to our friends and true to him. That is the kind of fidelity Paul meant by faith.

Sure that it is true

By faith Paul also means *belief*. He meant believing absolutely that Jesus is the Son of God and that everything he said is true.

When John Bunyan was in his days of doubt, one thing worried him more than anything else. He kept thinking that the Jews count their religion the best; the Mohammedans think their religion the best; what—he kept thinking—if Christianity be but a *think-so* too? Paul does not say, "I think"; he says, "I know."

How did Paul come to that certainty? He came in two ways. First, he had thought things out for himself. Paul wanted everyone to think. He said, "Test everything: hold fast what is good" (1 Thessalonians 5:21). A great Greek once said, "The unexamined life is the life not worth living." He meant that life can never be worth living until we think things out for ourselves and think things through. A lady who became a very famous scientist tells us that the beginning of her thirst for knowledge came when she was out for a walk with her father one day when quite young. Her father said to her, "Always have one principle in life—*Never believe what anyone tells you.*" He meant that she must never accept things just because someone told her, but must think everything out for herself. When the metallurgists are testing metals they test them in the laboratory; and they test them under strains many times as great as they will have to bear when they are in use. But they test them *before* they are put to use; it would be far too late to begin testing them when the strain came. It is too late to start thinking things out when the strain comes. We must think things out as soon as we possibly can, so that when the strains of life do come, there will be certain things which we know beyond doubt are true.

Second, Paul had actually met Jesus. He never thought of him as someone in a book. He thought of him as someone whom he knew and met every day and who gave him the guidance and the counsel and the strength he needed. Paul never said, "I know *what* I have believed"; he said, "I know *whom* I have believed" (2 Timothy 1:12). We can still meet Jesus, and when we do we are sure.

I will venture for thy name

By faith Paul also means *the willingness to take risks in order to be true to Jesus.* For him the great example of faith in action was Abraham.

Abraham was living a comfortable and successful life. God said to him, "You cannot really serve me here, amongst people who worship idols. If you are going to serve me, you must leave your home and your friends and your job; and you must go out into a strange and unknown country." Abraham might have said, "I cannot possibly take a risk like that." But "Abraham went out not knowing where he was to go" (Hebrews 11:8).

When John Bunyan was lying in prison, he was thinking of the execution that might come to him. He was naturally a little afraid; then he said to himself that it was shame to die with a pale face and tottering knees for such a cause as this. He imagined himself climbing up the ladder to the scaffold. He said to himself that he was quite willing now to jump off it into eternity. He prayed to Jesus to catch him as he leaped but if not, he said, "*I will venture for thy name.*" That is faith; faith is the willingness to take every risk in order to be true to Jesus.

Leaving things to God

To Paul faith really means *taking God at his word* and believing that everything he had said is true. For Paul, that worked backwards and forwards.

All his life Paul had been tortured by the feeling that he had not been as good as he should have been; and he did everything to try to *earn* God's forgiveness. Jesus had come to say that God is not a stern judge but that he is love. It took Paul a long time to learn that that is true. When he did he made the great discovery that the just shall live by faith. He learned that he could stop the unending effort to do the impossible and earn God's favour. He could simply go to him as he was because God is love.

Martin Luther had the same experience. He starved himself; he fasted; he lashed himself. He tried with might and main until he nearly broke his health altogether to *earn* God's favour. Once, to earn credit, he was struggling up the Sacred Staircase in Rome on his bare hands and knees. Suddenly a voice said to him, "The just shall live by faith." And he discovered that we cannot earn God's favour; God wants us because he loves us.

If you had asked Paul, "How do you know that?" he would have answered, "I know it because Jesus said it." For Paul, faith meant that he believed that what Jesus says about God is absolutely true, and he acted on that. All his life Paul had thought that God was a judge; Jesus said, "God so loved the world." Paul at last said, "I believe that what Jesus says is true; I believe that God loves me, even if I can never earn his love." That for Paul was faith.

Faith for Paul had its forward look, too. First, it laid on him a duty. It did not make life any less of an effort, because he knew that he must try his utmost to deserve God's love. But there was a difference now. He was trying now to be worthy of love; he was not trying any more to satisfy a judge.

Suppose we sit an examination. We know that we will get the marks that we have earned—*and no more*. There is a story about a boy who was trying to make a boat out of a piece of wood and could not get it to come right. Tired out and discouraged he went to bed, leaving the unfinished boat on a chair beside his bed. When he was sleeping his father came and saw it; and he took the chisel and the wood and shaped it into a perfect boat. When the boy woke in the morning, the thing that beat him had been done. He had done his best and, because his father loved him, he did not criticise the boat and give it a low mark; he took it, such as it was, and made it perfect.

That is the difference. If someone judges us, we get what we deserve and no more; if someone loves us, then if we do our best, even if it is not a very good best, love accepts what we have done. Paul was happy now because he knew that he was not trying to win the approval of a God who was an examiner, but to accept the love of a God who was a Father. He had to work his hardest to satisfy that love— but it was a joy now and not a terror any more.

Second, faith for Paul took away all fear. He knew that, whatever task lay ahead of him and whatever dangers threatened, God was with him. He had the great sense of never being alone and therefore of never being afraid.

In Christ

Over and over again Paul used a little phrase to tell people what he meant. That phrase was *in Christ*. He felt that his life and he himself were in Christ. Sometimes he put it the other way round and said that Christ was in him. Think of it this way. Think of the atmosphere, the air we breathe. We can say that we live because we live in the air and we also live because the air is in us. For Paul everything went back to Jesus. Faith for him was being absolutely loyal to Jesus. Faith for him was believing absolutely that what Jesus says is true. Faith for him meant staking everything on the adventure that what Jesus says about God and about life is absolutely to be trusted. Jesus had promised that, wherever he went, he would never leave him alone and that, whatever he had to do, he would never have to do it by himself. So Paul lived a life which he could only describe as *in Christ*.

"Yea, through life, death, through sorrow and through
      sinning
He shall suffice me, for he hath sufficed;
Christ is the end, for Christ was the beginning;
Christ the beginning, for the end was Christ."

CHAPTER TWENTY-SEVEN

This for Remembrance

The legacy of Paul

When a great man dies, he leaves something behind which continues to exist. His spirit continues to work in the world. The ending of Acts is symbolic. As we have seen, Acts is an unfinished story. We see Paul in prison but we never hear of his death. In a way that is a picture of the truth; for in one sense Paul did not die but lives on. More than 1900 years after his work on earth came to a close, Paul is still an active influence on the thought of men and on the belief of the Christian Church.

So then before we leave him, we must ask one more question. What were the great contributions that Paul made to Christian thought?

One in Christ Jesus

By far the greatest leap of originality that Paul made was his conception of all men being one in Christ Jesus. When he was writing to the Colossians, he spoke of the new Christian life in which "there cannot be Greek and Jew, circumcised and un-circumcised, barbarian, Scythian, slave, free man, but Christ is all and in all" (Colossians 3:11). When he was writing to the Galatians he said, "There is neither Jew nor Greek, there is neither slave nor free, there is neither male nor female; for you are all one in Christ Jesus" (Galatians 3:28). These are well-known and well-loved verses; but there is another passage, not so well-known but even more suggestive. In Colossians 1:27, 28 he speaks of "Christ ... the hope of glory. Him we proclaim, warning every man and teaching every man in all wisdom, that

we may present every man mature in Christ." The repetition of
the word "every" and the use of the word "all" in that passage
are extremely important. Paul wanted every man of every nation
of every class and of every condition for Jesus Christ. It is
difficult to realise what a tremendous leap of thought that was
for a Jew. He had been brought up to regard the Jews as the
chosen people. At best the Gentiles would be subjected to the
Jews and become their servants; at worst they would be completely wiped out.

It is well nigh impossible to overstress the exclusiveness of the
narrower and more nationalistic line of Jewish thought. The
great verse in Leviticus 19:18, "You shall not take vengeance or
bear any grudge against the sons of your own people, but you
shall love your neighbour as yourself," was taken as referring to
Jews and to Jews only; and the comment was added, "Against
others—that is, Gentiles—you may be vengeful and you may
bear a grudge." It was said that, "God loves only Israel of all
the nations he has made." Also, "God is the God of Israel and
not the God of the nations." A certain Rabbi said, "The best of
the Gentiles kill; the best of the serpents crush." "God will
judge the Israelites with one measure and the heathen with
another."

It was actually laid down that it was not legal to give a Gentile
mother help in the time of childbirth, because that would be
only to bring another Gentile into the world. "The nations are
as stubble or as straw which shall be burned or as chaff scattered
to the wind." "If a man repents God accepts him, but that
applies only to Israel and to no other nation." It is true that these
are the more bitter and the more exclusive voices; but it is also
true that that accent of exclusiveness ran through all Jewish
thought; and it is little less than a miracle that Paul, the Jewish
Rabbi, brought up in this gospel of exclusiveness, was the
man who conceived of a world where all men were one in
Christ.

In point of fact Paul lived in a world of barriers. To the Greek
the man who could not speak Greek was beyond the pale. To the
Roman the man of another race was automatically a barbarian.

To the philosopher the uneducated man was simply to be used as a tool. To the Jew even to educate a woman was to cast pearls before swine.

Into that world of barriers Paul brought this universal gospel. E. J. Goodspeed quotes a passage from Walter Lippmann. "As yet no teacher has ever appeared who was wise enough to know how to teach his wisdom to all mankind. In fact, the great teachers have attempted nothing so Utopian. They were quite well aware how difficult for most men is wisdom, and they have confessed frankly that the perfect life was for a select few. It is arguable, in fact, that the very idea of teaching the highest wisdom to all men is the recent notion of a humanitarian and romantically democratic age, and that it is quite foreign to the thought of the greatest teachers." But the American philosopher is wrong when he thinks that a modern idea; it is a Pauline idea; and the wonder is that it was an idea which haunted a man who was brought up in the most exclusive religion in the world.

That great idea still lies unrealised. We are still living in a world where there are barriers between class and class, between party and party, between nation and nation, between ideology and ideology, between colour and colour. An English writer tells how she paid a visit to America in the days when Paul Robson was famous as the greatest singer and one of the greatest actors in the world. She dined with him and his wife, and was thrilled. She went on to another American town and was telling her host and hostess about this experience. There was a certain frigidity in the reception of the story. "What's wrong?" she asked. Her friends replied, "If I were you, I would not talk too much about dining with Paul Robeson." "But," she said, ' he is the greatest singer and one of the greatest actors in the world." "That may be," answered her friends, "but *he is a nigger.*" That exclusiveness still exists.

Paul still points the way to us. There is nothing in the world which can draw men together into real unity other than Christianity. The only common brotherhood is to be found in the discovery that all men are sons of God. Unless that is realised, there can stretch before the world only more and more chaos and final disintegration. In this matter Paul stands out in front beckoning us on.

The independence of the Christian

Paul made another and a very different kind of contribution to thought. He laid down the independence of the Christian from the state and from all earthly powers. In this matter he was very wise and very sane. At all times he urged respect for the powers that be (Romans 13:1-7). No man was ever less of a revolutionary and an anarchist than Paul. Yet he saw quite clearly that there were limits beyond which the claim of the state could not go. He was the discoverer of the principle of religious liberty.

This again was new. There was no religious liberty in the Jewish religion. If a Jewish man was to marry a Gentile girl, or a Jewish girl a Gentile lad, the completely orthodox Jew would carry out the funeral of that Jewish lad or girl. By mixing with a faith other than the ancestral faith, they had rendered themselves nothing better than dead.

In Rome there was no such thing as religious liberty. Religions were divided into two kinds—licit and illicit. A licit religion was one which the state allowed; an illicit religion was one which was forbidden It was the cause of later persecution that Christianity was an illicit religion. In later times it was the demand that once a year every citizen should burn a pinch of incense on the altar of the reigning Emperor, who was regarded as a god. When he did so, he got a certificate—a *libellus*—to say so; and was then *libellaticus*—certificated. There is nothing like religious liberty there. When Paul met Roman magistrates he always met them with the greatest respect; but he always met them as an equal. If they insisted that he should be a good citizen, he heartily agreed; if they insisted that he should submit his way of worshipping God to them, he just as heartily refused.

Once again Paul laid down a great principle which has never died and which is specially dear to Scotland. James the Sixth did his best to reintroduce Romish ways into Scotland. The best men in the Church met him at Falkland. James Melville was reasonably and calmly presenting the case when the king interrupted, querulously demanding how they dared act in such a seditious way. Andrew Melville took him by the sleeve. "Sir," he said, "we will reverence your majesty always in public, but since we have this occasion to be with your majesty in private, and the truth is you are brought into extreme danger both of your life and crown, and with you the country and kirk of Christ are like to be wrecked, for not telling you the truth and giving you a faithful counsel, we must discharge our duty therein, or die traitors to both Christ and you. And therefore, sir, as divers times before, so now again, I must tell you there are two kings and two kingdoms in Scotland. There is Christ Jesus the King, and his kingdom is the kirk, whose subject King James the Sixth is, and of whose kingdom not a king, nor a lord, nor a head, but a member." There spoke the voice of religious liberty. That principle we owe to Paul and that principle we must maintain.

Jesus Christ is Lord

One other great contribution Paul made to our thought and belief. It is the conviction that Jesus Christ is Lord. It was Paul's dream, because he believed that it was God's dream, that there would come a day when every tongue would confess that Jesus Christ is Lord (Philippians 2:11). His favourite title for Jesus was Lord. To him the centre of the Christian religion is the Lordship of Christ. Here again Paul stands out in front beckoning us on.

What did he mean? He meant two things, to put it at its widest. First, he meant that Jesus Christ is unique, that there is no one like him in all the world, that he is the loveliest, the wisest, the greatest of all figures. And second, he meant that just because of that, we must be prepared to give him love and allegiance that we are not prepared to give to anyone else. Further, he meant that Jesus is Lord of all life, that there is not one part secular and one part sacred, one part where he is given his place and one part where he is shut out, but that every part of life, at home, at school, at sport, at business, on the streets and in the Church, must be dominated by the thought of the presence of, and by obedience to, Jesus Christ.

That is something we need to relearn. Our tendency nowadays is to meet with Jesus as an equal. We are quite prepared to talk things over with him. But, as someone has pointed out, Jesus did not say, "Discuss me"; he said, "Follow me." Once Charles Lamb and a band of literary men were sitting in a room playing a kind of game. They were pretending that they could summon back the great figures of the past and they were discussing what they would do if these figures came into the room. When they had exhausted the roll of history, Charles Lamb said with his shy stammer, "I can think of only one other. If Shakespeare were to come into this room, we would all rise up to do him honour; but if *he* were to come into this room, we would all kneel down and try to kiss the hem of his garment."

For Paul, Jesus was *Lord*. He was not a person with whom, or about whom, he argued. He was the one person who was Lord and King of his life and whom, without question, he obeyed.

The immortal ideas

Paul had the vision of a world for Christ. It is an ideal which is still in front of us. He insisted on the independence of Christ's Church. It is an ideal which we must maintain. He saw in Christ the Lord of life. It is an ideal which, in our own lives, we can realise.